Colonial America

Titles in the World History Series

The Age of Augustus
The Age of Exploration
The Age of Feudalism
The Age of Napoleon
The Age of Pericles
The Alamo
America in the 1960s
The American Frontier
The American Revolution
Ancient Chinese Dynasties
Ancient Greece
The Ancient Near East
Architecture
Aztec Civilization
The Battle of the
    Little Bighorn
The Black Death
The Byzantine Empire
Caesar's Conquest of Gaul
The California Gold Rush
The Chinese Cultural
    Revolution
The Civil Rights Movement
The Collapse of the
    Roman Republic
Colonial America
The Conquest of Mexico
The Constitution and the
    Founding of America
The Crimean War
The Crusades
The Cuban Missile Crisis
The Cuban Revolution
The Early Middle Ages
Egypt of the Pharaohs
Elizabethan England
The End of the Cold War
The Enlightenment
The French and Indian War
The French Revolution
The Glorious Revolution
The Great Depression
Greek and Roman
    Mythology
Greek and Roman Science
Greek and Roman Sport

Greek and Roman Theater
The History of Slavery
Hitler's Reich
The Hundred Years' War
The Incan Empire
The Industrial Revolution
The Inquisition
The Italian Renaissance
The Late Middle Ages
The Lewis and Clark
    Expedition
The Making of the Atom
    Bomb
The Mexican Revolution
The Mexican War of
    Independence
Modern Japan
The Mongol Empire
The Persian Empire
Prohibition
The Punic Wars
The Reagan Years
The Reformation
The Relocation of the North
    American Indian
The Renaissance
The Rise and Fall of the
    Soviet Union
The Roaring Twenties
The Roman Empire
The Roman Republic
Roosevelt and the New Deal
The Russian Revolution
Russia of the Tsars
The Scientific Revolution
The Spread of Islam
The Stone Age
The Titanic
Traditional Africa
Traditional Japan
The Travels of Marco Polo
Twentieth Century Science
The War of 1812
The Wars of the Roses
The Watts Riot
Women's Suffrage

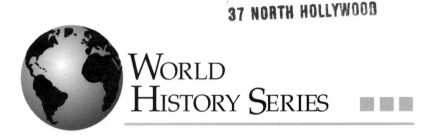

WORLD HISTORY SERIES

Colonial America

by
Bonnie L. Lukes

Y

Lucent Books, P.O. Box 289011, San Diego, CA 92198-9011

Library of Congress Cataloging-in-Publication Data

Lukes, Bonnie L., 19??–
     Colonial America / by Bonnie L. Lukes.
          p.   cm.—(World history series)
     Includes bibliographical references and index.
     Summary: Discusses various aspects of the Enlightenment
including its roots, philosophes, attacks on Christianity, revolt
against reason, campaigns to reform society, and legacy.
     ISBN 1-56006-321-1 (lib. : alk. paper)
     1. Eighteenth century—Juvenile literature. 2. Enlighten-
ment—Juvenile literature. 3. Europe—History—18th century—Juvenile literature [1. Enlightenment. 2. Eighteenth
century. 3. Europe—History—18th century.] I. Title. II. Series.
D286.D86 1999
940.2'53—dc21
                                                         98-8373
                                                            CIP
                                                            AC

Copyright 2000 by Lucent Books, Inc., P.O. Box 289011,
San Diego, California 92198-9011

Printed in the U.S.A.

Contents

Foreword   6
**Important Dates in the History of
Colonial America**   8

INTRODUCTION
Morning of America   10

CHAPTER 1
Staking a Claim in the New World   12

CHAPTER 2
The Fifth Jewel in the Crown: Virginia   21

CHAPTER 3
Pilgrims and Puritans: Plymouth and Massachusetts   32

CHAPTER 4
*Puritan Offshoots: Rhode Island, Connecticut,
and New Hampshire*   43

CHAPTER 5
Catholic Haven: Maryland   56

CHAPTER 6
A King's Reward: The Carolinas   67

CHAPTER 7
A Mixed Bag: New York and New Jersey   77

CHAPTER 8
The Holy Experiment: Pennsylvania and Delaware   87

CHAPTER 9
Georgia Makes Thirteen   98

EPILOGUE
An Emerging Nation   110

Notes   113
For Further Reading   117
Works Consulted   118
Index   123
Picture Credits   128
About the Author   128

'q

Foreword

Each year on the first day of school, nearly every history teacher faces the task of explaining why his or her students should study history. One logical answer to this question is that exploring what happened in our past explains how the things we often take for granted—our customs, ideas, and institutions—came to be. As statesman and historian Winston Churchill put it, "Every nation or group of nations has its own tale to tell. Knowledge of the trials and struggles is necessary to all who would comprehend the problems, perils, challenges, and opportunities which confront us today." Thus, a study of history puts modern ideas and institutions in perspective. For example, though the founders of the United States were talented and creative thinkers, they clearly did not invent the concept of democracy. Instead, they adapted some democratic ideas that had originated in ancient Greece and with which the Romans, the British, and others had experimented. An exploration of these cultures, then, reveals their very real connection to us through institutions that continue to shape our daily lives.

Another reason often given for studying history is the idea that lessons exist in the past from which contemporary societies can benefit and learn. This idea, although controversial, has always been an intriguing one for historians. Those who agree that society can benefit from the past often quote philosopher George Santayana's famous statement, "Those who cannot remember the past are condemned to repeat it." Historians who subscribe to Santayana's philosophy believe that, for example, studying the events that led up to the major world wars or other significant historical events would allow society to chart a different and more favorable course in the future.

Just as difficult as convincing students to realize the importance of studying history is the search for useful and interesting supplementary materials that present historical events in a context that can be easily understood. The volumes in Lucent Books' World History Series attempt to present a broad, balanced, and penetrating view of the march of history. Ancient Egypt's important wars and rulers, for example, are presented against the rich and colorful backdrop of Egyptian religious, social, and cultural developments. The series engages the reader by enhancing historical events with these cultural contexts. For example, in *Ancient Greece,* the text covers the role of women in that society. Slavery is discussed in *The Roman Empire,* as well as how slaves earned their freedom. The numerous and varied aspects of every-day life in these and other societies are explored in each volume of the series. Additionally, the series covers the major political, cultural, and philosophical ideas as the torch of civilization is passed from ancient Mesopotamia and Egypt, through Greece, Rome, Medieval Europe, and other world cultures, to the modern day.

The material in the series is formatted in a thorough, precise, and organized manner. Each volume offers the reader a comprehensive and clearly written overview of an important historical event or period. The topic under discussion is placed in a broad, historical context. For example, *The Italian Renaissance* begins with a discussion of the High Middle Ages and the loss of central control that allowed certain Italian cities to develop artistically. The book ends by looking forward to the Reformation and interpreting the societal changes that grew out of the Renaissance. Thus, students are not only involved in an historical era, but also enveloped by the events leading up to that era and the events following it.

One important and unique feature in the World History Series is the primary and secondary source quotations that richly supplement each volume. These quotes are useful in a number of ways. First, they allow students access to sources they would not normally be exposed to because of the difficulty and obscurity of the original source. The quotations range from interesting anecdotes to farsighted cultural perspectives and are drawn from historical witnesses both past and present. Second, the quotes demonstrate how and where historians themselves derive their information on the past as they strive to reach a consensus on historical events. Lastly, all of the quotes are footnoted, familiarizing students with the citation process and allowing them to verify quotes and/or look up the original source if the quote piques their interest.

Finally, the books in the World History Series provide a detailed launching point for further research. Each book contains a bibliography specifically geared toward student research. A second, annotated bibliography introduces students to all the sources the author consulted when compiling the book. A chronology of important dates gives students an overview, at a glance, of the topic covered. Where applicable, a glossary of terms is included.

In short, the series is designed not only to acquaint readers with the basics of history, but also to make them aware that their lives are a part of an ongoing human saga. Perhaps they will then come to the same realization as famed historian Arnold Toynbee. In his monumental work, *A Study of History,* he wrote about becoming aware of history flowing through him in a mighty current, and of his own life "welling like a wave in the flow of this vast tide."

IMPORTANT DATES IN THE HISTORY OF COLONIAL AMERICA

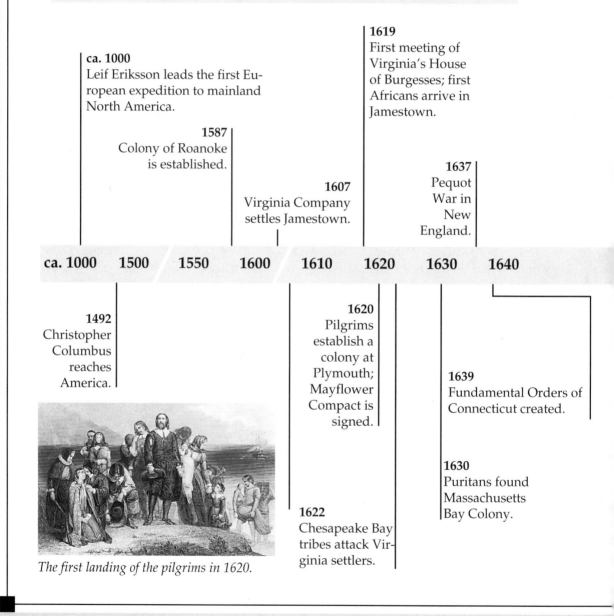

ca. 1000
Leif Eriksson leads the first European expedition to mainland North America.

1587
Colony of Roanoke is established.

1607
Virginia Company settles Jamestown.

1619
First meeting of Virginia's House of Burgesses; first Africans arrive in Jamestown.

1637
Pequot War in New England.

ca. 1000	1500	1550	1600	1610	1620	1630	1640

1492
Christopher Columbus reaches America.

1620
Pilgrims establish a colony at Plymouth; Mayflower Compact is signed.

1639
Fundamental Orders of Connecticut created.

1630
Puritans found Massachusetts Bay Colony.

1622
Chesapeake Bay tribes attack Virginia settlers.

The first landing of the pilgrims in 1620.

1670
Charlestown
(Charleston),
South Carolina,
is founded.

1676
Bacon's Rebellion in Virginia.

1689
Leisler's Rebellion in
New York; William and
Mary assume the throne
in England.

1660
Monarchy is restored in England.

1642–1649
Civil war in
England;
Monarchy
overthrown.

1732
Georgia is
founded by
James
Oglethorpe
and others.

1649
Maryland Assembly
passes Toleration Act.

1640	1650	1660	1670	1680	1690	1700	1750

1663
Charles II grants a
proprietary char-
ter for a colony in
the Carolinas.

1643
New England
Confederation
is formed.

1675
King Philip's War begins in
New England.

1692–1693
Salem witchcraft trials.

1688
Glorious Revolution occurs
in England.

1682
Quaker migration to Pennsylvania
begins under proprietary charter to
William Penn; Penn obtains
Delaware from James, duke of York.

1677
Culpepper's
Rebellion in North Carolina.

Morning of America

America is the only country in the world that was founded entirely by immigrants. "What we mean by the history of the American people," writes Pulitzer Prize–winning historian Samuel E. Morison, "is the history . . . of immigrants from other continents."[1]

Tens of thousands of years before Columbus discovered the New World, the first immigrants had migrated there, probably from Asia. By the time Columbus arrived, 15 to 20 million of these Native Americans lived in the Western Hemisphere. However, only a few million inhabited what is now the

Columbus's discovery of the New World in 1492 marked the beginning of large-scale, European colonization of the Americas.

United States and Canada when the English arrived to establish Jamestown, Virginia.

The immigrants to Virginia were only a minute part of the great wave of English settlers that would follow. These courageous trailblazers brought with them England's traditions and institutions. They soon found, however, that the old ways did not work in the New World. Unfamiliar challenges confronted them. As one of them wrote, they had "all things to do, as in the beginning of the world."[2]

Two major obstacles threatened the colonists' survival. One was the untamed land itself; the other was the Native Americans who, understandably, saw the colonists as intruders in their homeland.

But despite the dangers and hardships, immigrants continued to come from England as well as all across Europe. They came from Sweden, Germany, France, and the Netherlands. They brought their dreams to what they saw as a clean, untouched place where they could make a fresh start. Most came filled with hope. Not all immigrants came by choice, however. Many were brought from Africa in chains—arriving not in hope, but in despair. Yet no matter how people reached the shores of the New World, or whatever their reasons for coming, each group stamped the emerging American character with its own indelible imprint.

How these varied peoples—brought to a new land either by fate or by their own yearnings for a better life—laid the building blocks for a great nation is the story of colonial America.

1 Staking a Claim in the New World

At 2:00 A.M. on the moonlit morning of October 12, 1492, a lookout on Christopher Columbus's ship the *Pinta* shouted, *"Tierra! Tierra!"* ("Land! Land!"). Columbus was unaware that he had stumbled upon a new world that comprised two new continents: North and South America. And he certainly could not have guessed that his discovery would lead to the planting of thirteen English colonies that would one day become a great nation.

However, Spain—not England—would be the first European country to stake formal claims in the Americas. Half the territory of what would become the continental United States belonged to Spain before England attempted its first settlement. At this time England, unlike Spain, was still struggling to become a unified country.

ENGLAND ON THE EVE OF COLONIZATION

Briefly in 1509 it appeared that England had achieved enough national unity to challenge Spain for a share of the New World. But then Henry VIII, the ruling monarch, threw the country into turmoil when he separated from the Catholic Church and established the Protestant Church of England. The resulting internal religious wars between Protestants and Catholics, plus an ongoing war with powerful Catholic Spain, kept England occupied until the mid-1500s. By that time England had grown stronger, and the Crown's advisers urged colonizing in the New World.

ENGLAND'S MOTIVES FOR COLONIZING

Multiple factors prompted England to establish colonies in America. One was the economy. Changes in England's agricultural system and the loss of a market for woolen cloth, England's primary export, had caused widespread unemployment. Destitute beggars roamed the English countryside. Population had doubled. England viewed colonization as a way to rid itself of its poor and its surplus population. A desire to spread Christianity and to check the power of Spain were also strong incentives. And, as English geographer

Columbus's discoveries allowed Spain to gain a significant advantage in colonizing the New World.

and scholar Richard Hakuylt pointed out, colonies could furnish England with a source of raw materials and provide a new market for the sale of finished products.

Nevertheless, by 1558, when Elizabeth I became queen, England still had made no attempt to plant a colony in the New World. Elizabeth would lead the way.

FAILED EFFORTS

Under Queen Elizabeth, England defeated Spain's powerful naval fleet—the Spanish Armada. The new queen also restored a measure of religious harmony to the country. She also encouraged the large trading companies by granting them charters that gave them monopolies over English trade in specific areas. In this way, England endeavored to establish its first colony in North America.

In 1584 Elizabeth granted Sir Walter Raleigh a charter that gave him title to the land of "Virginia"—the name given to the area that stretched from Maine to Florida along the Atlantic Coast. A crew explored the Chesapeake Bay area and approved Roanoke Island (in what is now North Carolina) as an acceptable site for a colony. The first group of settlers were unsuccessful and returned to England after only one year.

A second attempt was made in 1587 when Raleigh sent 121 settlers, including women and children, to Roanoke. This effort might have succeeded if the colony had been supported from home; however, that was the year of the Spanish Armada, and England needed all of its resources on the home front. Three years passed before anyone thought to check on Roanoke. By that time the entire colony had disappeared—including little

Explorers investigating the disappearance of the English settlement at Roanoke found only the word "Croatoan" carved on a tree.

Virginia Dare, the first child of English parents born in America. Historian Samuel E. Morison writes,

> Nobody knows what became of the "Lost Colony." The best guess is that some starved to death, and others were killed by the Indians, who adopted the surviving children. To this day the Croatoan (now called Lumbee) Indians of Robeson County, North Carolina, maintain that the blood of Raleigh's colonists runs in their veins.[3]

The failure of Roanoke meant that England would enter the seventeenth century still without a colony in the New World. But this would soon change.

A New Monarch and a New Approach

The Roanoke experience made it clear that colonizing financed and promoted by a single individual like Raleigh did not work. Consequently, the joint-stock companies, promoted by Elizabeth I for trading purposes, now went into the colonizing business. These companies were made up of investors, similar to today's corporations; their primary objective was to make a profit.

Companies had to be chartered by the Crown. The ruling monarch granted them the land, but the companies had to bear the expense of governing the colonies they established. The monarch retained control, however, by appointing a royal council that would have general supervision over the colonies. Charters were cherished by colonial Americans because a charter guaranteed the extension of their rights and privileges as English citizens.

In 1603 James I became king. Three years later he issued a joint charter to two companies, the London Company and the Plymouth Company, authorizing them to settle the territory known as Virginia. The Plymouth Company tried to found a colony on the Kennebec River in Maine but failed. However, the London Company, or as it was more often called, the Virginia Company, would establish England's first permanent colony in North America.

JAMESTOWN: THE BEGINNING

On December 20, 1606, three small vessels departed from England bound for Virginia. The 144 who sailed—all of them men—were, for the most part, "soft-handed" gentlemen who had never been required to work. Future colonies would be founded by reformers seeking a perfect

Under James I, England was able to establish its first permanent settlements in North America.

society, by people fleeing from religious persecution, or by those searching for a better life and an opportunity to own land. But this first group contained mostly adventurers who expected to find gold and then return to England with their riches. Only a precious few were craftsmen such as carpenters or bricklayers. In *Our Earliest Colonial Settlements*, historian Charles M. Andrews writes,

> The promoters had not yet realized that a colony to be permanent should root itself in the soil, that it should be self-perpetuating and self-sustaining . . . raising its own food instead of waiting for supplies from home. It took Englishmen a long time to learn that a settlement to be successful had to rest upon a more certain foundation than the desire for wealth.[4]

The voyage took four months. Thirty-nine men died at sea. One of the passengers, Captain John Smith, was accused of speaking against the government and was put in irons.

ARRIVAL IN THE NEW WORLD

At the first port of call, the survivors opened a sealed box that contained the names of seven men who were to serve on the local council. When it was discovered that John Smith was one of those named, he was released from confinement.

The council's first task was to choose a suitable site. Despite the company's warning not to settle "in a low and moist place because it will prove unheathful,"[5] the councilmen selected a site on a peninsula of the James River. It was not a wise choice. Jamestown would turn into a swamp in the summer and become a breeding ground for malaria.

These first arrivals were not equipped to deal with the physical and mental hardships that lay ahead. Moreover, they had little incentive to work. The land belonged to the Virginia Company, and the

---

The First Year at Jamestown

George Percy, who later replaced John Smith as president of the Jamestown council, sailed on the first voyage to the Virginia Colony. He recorded the details of the voyage, the landing, and the hardships of the first year. Editor David Hawke included Percy's commentary in his book U.S. Colonial History: Readings and Documents.

"The 15th day of June we had built and finished our fort, which was triangle-wise, having three bulwarks at every corner like a half moon, and four or five pieces of artillery mounted in them. We had made ourselves sufficiently strong for these savages. We had also sown most of our corn on two mountains. . . .

Monday, the two and twentieth of June . . . Captain Newport . . . departed from James Fort for England . . . leaving us very bare and scanty of victuals . . . and in danger of the savages. . . .

Our men were destroyed with cruel diseases as swellings, fluxes, burning fevers, and by wars, and some departed [died] suddenly, but for the most part they died of mere famine. There were never Englishmen left in a foreign country in such misery as we were in this new-discovered Virginia. . . . Our food was but a small can of barley sod [boiled or soaked] in water to five men a day, our drink cold water taken out of the river, which was at a flood very salt[y], at a low tide full of slime and filth, which was the destruction of many of our men. Thus we lived for . . . five months in this miserable distress, not having five able men to man our bulwarks upon any occasion. . . . Our men night and day groaning in every corner of the fort most pitiful to hear. If there were any conscience in men, it would make their hearts to bleed to hear the . . . outcries of our sick men without relief every night and day . . . some departing out of the world, many times three or four in a night; in the mornings their bodies trailed out of their cabins like dogs to be buried."

Many of Jamestown's early settlers were "gentlemen" who were not used to the rigors of manual labor.

settlers themselves were no more than employees. Each man received the same pay whether he worked much or little. Food was all around them in the form of fish and game, but few of them knew how to fish or hunt. The ones who did were too fearful of the native inhabitants to venture into the woods.

THE AMERICAN SCENE

The Native Americans around Jamestown belonged to the Algonquian language group. They were led by Powhatan, who controlled, or at least had influence over, some thirty tribes. He saw the whites as potential allies against enemy tribes, but he also viewed them as interlopers who had to be carefully watched.

However, despite some Native American hostility, few of these first settlers were killed by Indians. The enemy was famine and sickness. And it is doubtful that those few who survived the first winter could have done so without Powhatan's help. George Percy, a future president of the council, wrote at the time, "It pleased God, after a while, to send those people which were our mortall enemies to releeve us with victuals, [such] as Bread, Corne, Fish, and Flesh in great plentie . . . otherwise e [would have] all perished."[6] By January only thirty-eight men remained alive. "Such famine and sickness," Captain John Smith wrote, "that the living were scarce able to bury the dead."[7] Out of this chaos, Smith emerged as the real leader.

Captain John Smith

In September John Smith was elected president of the Jamestown council. He established a rapport with the Indians that enabled him to buy corn for the colony. Captured by the Algonquians on one of his trading expeditions, he later wrote that Pocahontas—the twelve-year-old daughter of Chief Powhatan—had saved him from being killed. Smith achieved a working relationship with Powhatan that led to relatively peaceful dealings between the settlers and Indians.

More men arrived in Jamestown, but few were the practical, hardworking sort the settlement needed. Smith despised the many shiftless drones who contributed nothing to the colony's success. He made and enforced the rule that "he who works not, eats not."[8] Men grumbled, but only a dozen out of approximately two hundred died during that second winter of 1608–1609. The low death toll was due to Smith's leadership.

However, Smith began to overstep his authority. When councilmen died or returned to England, he refused to appoint new ones. The dwindling number of councilmen accused Smith of assuming dictatorial powers and began a campaign to get rid of him. Smith was suffering in-

tense pain from a wound sustained in a gunpowder explosion, and in the summer of 1609 his enemies used that as an excuse to ship him back to England.

The Virginia Company Reorganizes

But John Smith had awakened the Virginia Company to the need for change. Under a new charter, the company encouraged immigration by offering free

Captain John Smith's relationship with Powhatan and his daughter Pocahontas led to relatively peaceful dealings between settlers and Indians.

CHIEF POWHATAN PLEADS FOR PEACE

For the most part, Powhatan and John Smith managed to coexist peacefully, but in a speech to Smith, Powhatan voiced fears for his people—fears that proved to be prophetic. His speech is included in 100 Key Documents in American Democracy, *edited by Peter B. Levy.*

"Why should you take by force that from us which you can have by love? Why should you destroy us, who have provided you with food? What can you get by war? . . . What is the cause of your jealousy? You see us unarmed, and willing to supply your wants if you will come in a friendly manner, and not with swords and guns, as to invade an enemy. I am not so simple, as not to know it is better to eat good meat, . . . sleep quietly with my women and children . . . laugh and be merry with the English; and, being their friend to have copper, hatchets, and whatever else I want, than to [flee], to lie cold in the woods, feed upon acorns . . . and to be so hunted that I cannot rest, eat or sleep. . . . I, therefore, exhort you to peaceable councils; and above all, I insist that the guns and swords, the cause of all our jealousy and uneasiness, be removed and sent away."

passage in exchange for seven years of unpaid labor. Immigrants who took advantage of this opportunity were called indentured servants. Those who could pay their own way also agreed to work for the company for seven years, but they received one share of company stock. Company profits would be divided evenly at the end of the seven years, and the shareholders would receive a bonus of one hundred acres of land.

The Virginia Company also abolished the local council and instituted a powerful one-man government. The king appointed Lord De La Warre, governor and Sir Thomas Gates, lieutenant governor. In the spring of 1609, Gates sailed for Virginia in a fleet of nine vessels that carried five hundred men, women, and children. But a hurricane scattered the fleet, and Gates's ship was stranded in Bermuda. The others made it to Jamestown, bringing four hundred more people to a place where everyone was already starving.

STARVING TIMES

With John Smith's return to England, the colonists' harmonious relationship with the Native Americans ended. The Indians repeatedly attacked the fort and refused to trade with the settlers. Men could not leave the fort to work the land or search

After John Smith's departure, relationships with the Indians deteriorated and nearly led to the destruction of Jamestown.

for food because the Indians lay in wait. Death from malaria and dysentery was rampant. The people had little food, and according to George Percy—who had replaced Smith—they survived on whatever they could find, "even the very skins of our horses."[9] One man was executed for cannibalism.

When Lieutenant Governor Gates finally reached Jamestown in May 1610, he found only 60 survivors. Unprepared for such devastation, Gates had brought another 175 settlers and only a small amount of food. Within two weeks he decided to abandon the settlement. But just as he was leaving with all of the colonists, Governor De La Warre arrived with fresh supplies. On the governor's order, Gates and the discouraged colonists returned to Jamestown. They would try again.

2 The Fifth Jewel in the Crown: Virginia

The near failure of Jamestown prompted the Virginia Company to establish military rule in the colony. Settlers' rights—which had been guaranteed under the original charter—were suspended, and Governor De La Warre instituted a strict new code of laws. When Sir Thomas Dale, a former soldier, replaced De La Warre as governor, he not only enforced the harsh new laws but also added more. These published laws soon became known as "Dale's Code." Twenty offenses were punishable by death. One, regarding swearing, decreed that

> no man [shall] blaspheme God's holy name upon pain . . . of severe punishment for the first offense so committed and for the second [offense] to have a bodkin [dagger] thrust through his tongue; and . . . for the third time so offending he shall be brought to a martial court and there receive censure of death for his offense.[10]

No more famines occurred under this rigid system, but sickness and death continued to take a high toll. Newcomers now included skilled workers such as carpenters, but the Virginia Company—having failed to produce an export product that would yield a profit for its investors—was now in financial trouble.

A Colony "Built upon Smoke"

The colonists had experimented with numerous export possibilities, all of which failed. They tried exporting timber, but the cost of shipping was too high. They imported silkworms hoping to start a silk industry, but they soon realized that such an industry, even if successful, would take years to show a profit. Then, thinking the Virginia soil ideal for growing grapes, they imported grapevine cuttings from France—only to find that Virginia's climate was too wet for grape vineyards. It was not, however, too wet for growing tobacco plants. And in England, tobacco was in great demand because merchants had to import it from the Spanish West Indies at exorbitant prices. The Native Americans grew tobacco, but the English found its quality unacceptable.

After much experimenting, a colonist named John Rolfe succeeded in developing a high-quality tobacco, and Virginia sent its first shipment to England in 1614. Within four years, fifty thousand pounds of tobacco a year were being exported. Charles I would later urge the Virginians to develop a more substantial product, complaining that the colony was "wholly built upon smoke, tobacco being the only [product] it hath produced."[11] But John Rolfe's tobacco plant had guaranteed Virginia's survival. Rolfe was also responsible for a welcome interlude of peace between the settlers and the Indians.

The Capture of Pocahontas

The Virginia colonists did not forget that Powhatan had kept the Jamestown settlers virtual prisoners in their fort. After Governor De La Warre's arrival, they set out to make the "bloodye infidelles" pay. They sent groups to destroy entire Indian villages and slaughter the inhabitants. Finally, in 1613 the colonists kidnapped and held hostage Pocahontas, the grown daughter of Chief Powhatan—the same Pocahontas who at age twelve had saved John Smith.

Pocahontas remained a prisoner for one year. During that time, she and John Rolfe fell in love. When Pocahontas returned to her village, she told her father she preferred to stay among the English. Powhatan agreed, and in 1614 Rolfe and Pocahontas were married. The marriage forged a peace between the Jamestown settlers and the Native Americans that lasted until Powhatan's death. This peace, combined with the success of tobacco, made the Virginia Company optimistic about the future prosperity of both the colony and the company.

The Virginia Company Struggles to Stay Afloat

By 1616—Governor Dale's last year in the colony—the high hopes of the Virginia Company had not materialized. Tobacco was profitable, but the number of inha-

Profits from the export of tobacco guaranteed the survival of the Virginia Company and the settlement at Jamestown.

John Rolfe's marriage to the Indian princess Pocahontas brought peace between the colonists and the neighboring Native American tribes.

bitants in Virginia was still only "three hundred and fifty-one persons—a small nomber to advance so great a worke."[12]

The Virginia Company was near financial collapse. In addition, its stockholders could not agree on the best way to manage the colony. The more liberal faction wanted to replace Virginia's harsh military rule with "just laws for the happy guiding and governing of the people."[13] The liberals eventually gained control and elected Sir George Yeardley to be Virginia's new governor.

A YEAR TO BE REMEMBERED

Governor Yeardley took office in 1619. Martial law was abolished, and individual liberty was restored. To attract more settlers and ensure faster economic success, the Virginia Company also instituted the "headright system." Under this system, those who paid their own way received fifty acres of land outright plus another fifty for every person they brought with them. If a man brought himself, his wife, and his two children, for

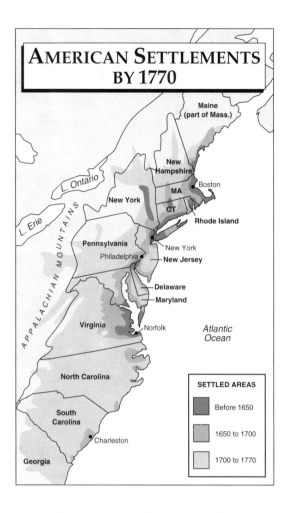

AMERICAN SETTLEMENTS BY 1770

Maine
(part of Mass.)

New Hampshire

Boston

MA

New York

CT

Rhode Island

L. Ontario

L. Erie

APPALACHIAN MOUNTAINS

Pennsylvania

Philadelphia

New York

New Jersey

Delaware

Maryland

Virginia

Norfolk

Atlantic Ocean

North Carolina

South Carolina

Charleston

Georgia

SETTLED AREAS

Before 1650

1650 to 1700

1700 to 1770

example, he was entitled to two hundred acres. Even an unmarried woman could receive fifty acres if she paid her own passage.

The company also instructed the governor to establish a general assembly that would include colonial representatives (called burgesses) elected by the settlers. The Virginia Company declared that by divine guidance, it intended "to settle such a forme of government ther as may bee to the greatest benefitt and comfort of the people and whereby all Injustice, grevance, and oppression may bee pre-

vented."[14] This representative assembly turned out to be the beginning of self-government in colonial America.

Ironically, only a month after the formation of an institution that guaranteed justice and freedom, the seeds of another institution arrived in Jamestown—one that would deny those rights to certain Americans. The Virginia Company noted in its records, "About the last of August came in a dutch man of warre that sold us twenty Negars."[15] By the end of the century, slavery would be firmly entrenched in colonial America.

Women also came to Jamestown that year—ninety of them—sent by the company as prospective wives for the settlers. Carefully screened, these were young women of good reputation. They lived in the homes of married couples where they could receive suitors if they chose. A successful suitor was required to reimburse the company for the expense of bringing his bride to the colony. The cost: 120 pounds of tobacco.

Others came, or were sent, to Virginia because of the wretched living conditions in England in 1619 brought about by low wages and high unemployment. When an English official suggested that England send "their poore with whome they are pestered into Virginia,"[16] one hundred boys and girls were sent as apprentices.

Indentured servants also came in greater numbers from many levels of English society. Some were criminals released from jail on the condition that they go to the colonies; others had once held high social positions but were down on their luck. Servitude was not an easy life, but it offered a way to improve social status by becoming a landowner—an opportunity not available in England. Virginia's middle class would emerge from this group.

At the end of 1619, Virginia was prospering despite the continuing high death rate that kept the population small. (In one year over a thousand people died, either on the way over or in the colony.) The financial condition of the Virginia Company remained precarious, but the future held new promise. Then, in 1622, catastrophe struck.

MASSACRE AND BANKRUPTCY

The colonists—seeking more land on which to grow the profitable tobacco plant—had begun establishing settlements along the James River outside of Jamestown. Meanwhile, Chief Powhatan had died and Opechancanough had replaced him as leader of the Chesapeake Bay tribes. Opechancanough hated the English settlers, and as he watched them encroach farther on Indian land, his anger grew.

The arrival of twenty black slaves aboard a Dutch ship in August 1619 marked the beginning of slavery in the English colonies.

Opechancanough began organizing great numbers of warriors, and on March 22, 1622, he and his army struck. "They basely and barbarously murdered," a survivor wrote, "not sparing either age or sex, man, woman, or child."[17] Within a few hours, 347 colonists were slaughtered.

Opechancanough's deadly and well-organized attack nearly destroyed the colony completely. A colonist wrote back to England: "The last massacre killed all our country; beside[s] them they killed, they burst the heart of all the rest."[18]

VIRGINIA BECOMES A ROYAL COLONY

The Virginia Company never recovered from the massacre's effects. On May 24, 1624, the king revoked its charter, and Virginia became a royal colony. This made the monarchy responsible for the day-to-day managing of Virginia's affairs. Charles I, who had succeeded King James, proclaimed, "The Government of the Collonie of Virginia shall . . . depend upon our selfe, and not be committed to anie Company or corporation."[19]

THE HOUSE OF BURGESSES IS FIRMLY ESTABLISHED

The colonists feared that under direct royal rule, the harsh government that had existed under "Dale's Code" would be restored. Their apprehension appeared valid when the king dissolved the House of Burgesses and appointed a royal gover-

nor with absolute power. However, a succession of royal governors found that a colonial assembly was necessary if they hoped to receive any cooperation from the colonists. Therefore, in 1639 the king instructed the royal governor to call the assembly into session

> as formerly, once a year or oftener if urgent occasion shall require, to summon the Burgesses . . . which together with the governor and Council shall have power to make acts and laws for the government . . . correspondent as near as may be to the laws of England.[20]

The king's action set a precedent that would assure a representative colonial assembly in each of the thirteen colonies.

VIRGINIA GROWS AND PROSPERS

By this time Virginia's population had increased to over seven thousand, and eight new counties had been created. Colonists had begun building better houses and planting gardens and orchards—an indication that they had come to stay. They concentrated on growing and exporting tobacco. At this point the settlers did most of their own work—assisted by white indentured servants who would later become tobacco farmers themselves. There were still only about 250 blacks in Virginia.

Despite Virginia's increasing stability, it remained a frontier colony. In 1644 the Indians, led by the aging Opechancanough, made one last stand against the

REPORT ON THE 1622 MASSACRE

After Chief Opechan-canough's devastating attack on the settlers in March 1622, the Virginia Company sent an official report to its investors. The following excerpts are from Opposing Viewpoints in American History, *edited by William Dudley.*

"[Opechancanough], the King of these savages, about the middle of March last, . . . [sent word] that he held the peace . . . so firm [that] the sky should sooner fall than it dissolve. Yea, such was the treacherous dissimulation [deception] of that people who then contrived our destruction, that even two days before the massacre, some of our men were guided through the woods by them in safety. . . . And . . . on the Friday morning (the fatal day) the twenty-second of March, . . . as on other days before, they came unarmed into our houses . . . to sell and trade with us for glass, beads, and other trifles. . . . In some places, they sat down at breakfast with our people at their tables . . . and barbarously murdered, not sparing either age or sex, man, woman, or child, so sudden in their cruel execution that few . . . discerned the weapon or blow that brought them to destruction. . . . They also slew many of our people then at their . . . work . . . in the fields . . . some in planting corn and tobacco, some in gardening, some in making brick, building, sawing, . . . they well knowing in what places and quarters each of our men were. . . . And by this means that fatal Friday morning, there [they] fell under the bloody and barbarous hands of that perfidious and inhuman people, contrary to all laws of God and men, of nature and nations, three hundred forty seven men, women and children, most by their own weapons. . . . Thus have you seen the particulars of this massacre, wherein treachery and cruelty have done their worst to us, or rather to themselves . . . because betraying innocence never rests unpunished."

Virginians, attacking and killing three hundred people. But the settlers rallied and drove them back. Defeated, the Indians signed a peace treaty under which they ceded much of their land to the settlers. Unlike Opechancanough's earlier attack, this one had little effect on the progress of the colony.

Housing in Virginia in 1687

By 1687 Virginia had advanced beyond its crude beginnings at Jamestown. A Frenchman exiled to Virginia because of his religious beliefs wrote this description of housing in the colony. It is included in The Old Dominion in the Seventeenth Century, *edited by Warren M. Billings.*

"Some people in this country are comfortably housed; the farmers' houses are built entirely of wood, the roofs being made of small boards of chestnut, as are also the walls. Those who have some means, cover them inside with a coating of mortar in which they use oyster-shells for lime; it is as white as snow, so that although they look ugly from the outside, where only the wood can be seen, they are very pleasant inside, with convenient windows and openings. They have started making bricks in quantities, and I have seen several houses where the walls were entirely made of them. Whatever their rank, and I know not why, they build only two rooms with some closets on the ground floor, and two rooms in the attic above; but they build several like this, according to their means. They build also a separate kitchen, a separate house for the Christian slaves, one for the negro slaves, and several to dry the tobacco, so that when you come to the home of a person of some means, you think you are entering a fairly large village. There are no stables because they never lock up their cattle. Indeed few of the houses have a lock, for nothing is ever stolen."

Growing Pains

By 1660 Virginia's population had grown to around thirty thousand, and a new kind of immigrant began arriving. Many of these were the younger sons of England's middle-class gentry. In England only first-born sons were allowed to inherit land, so younger sons were eager to come to Virginia where they could own land. Families like the Washingtons and the Jeffersons, who would provide Virginia's political leadership in the eighteenth century, emerged from this group.

Although the huge plantations would not come into existence until the eighteenth century, wealthy tobacco planters already had control of the coastal tobacco lands. This created problems in the 1670s, when large numbers of indentured servants completed their service and demanded the land that had been promised to them. These former servants, along with the poorer farmers, were forced to migrate into the interior, where Indian tribes still posed a serious threat. The result was hostility between the backcountry settlers and the wealthy planters.

BACON'S REBELLION

The frontiersmen repeatedly asked Sir William Berkeley, Virginia's royal governor, for help in fighting the Native Americans, but he refused to send aid. The frontier planters and farmers said that Berkeley and his followers, the wealthy planters and office holders, were more interested in protecting their lucrative fur trade with the Indians than in protecting families in the backcountry. Finally, after a destructive Indian attack in 1676, a young aristocratic frontier planter named Nathaniel Bacon took matters into his own hands.

Bacon first requested a commission from Governor Berkeley that would allow him to launch all-out warfare against the Native Americans. "I would . . . go in defense of the country against all Indians in general," Bacon wrote Berkeley, "for . . . they [are] all our enemies."[21] The commission was refused, but Bacon was not deterred. He led an army of frontiersmen against peaceful as well as hostile Indian tribes. When Berkeley branded him a traitor to the king, Bacon angrily marched his frontier army to Jamestown and burned it to the ground. The House of Burgesses, emboldened by Bacon's action, passed reform measures to increase popular participation in colonial government and to curb the political power of the wealthy planters. However, the rebellion ended when Bacon died from a sudden illness.

BURNING OF JAMESTOWN.

Bacon angrily marches his frontier army to Jamestown and burns it to the ground.

Nathaniel Bacon became a legendary hero to the common people. Although most of the new laws were repealed after Bacon's death, the issue of a more democratic political process had been raised in Virginia for the first time. Nathaniel Ba-

---

THE APPRENTICESHIP OF ORPHANS

In January 1620 the Virginia leaders reported to the Virginia Company's investors in England regarding the treatment of orphaned children sent from London to the colony. This excerpt is from The Annals of America, *edited by Mortimer J. Adler.*

"One hundred children . . . were the last spring . . . transported by the Virginia Company from the City of London unto Virginia, and . . . for the transportation and appareling of [these] children . . . 500 pounds was paid unto the . . . Company. . . . For the good of the same children . . . it is . . . ordered . . . that every [one] . . . shall be educated and brought up in some good trade and profession, whereby they may be enabled to get their living and maintain themselves when they shall attain . . . four-and-twenty years, or be out of their apprenticeships, which shall endure at the least seven years if they so long live.

And, further, that . . . the boys at their ages of one-and-twenty years or upward, and the maids or girls at their age of one-and-twenty years, or day of marriage, which shall first happen, shall have freely given and allotted unto them fifty acres of land apiece in Virginia. . . .

And . . . that at the expiration of their . . . apprenticeships . . . the said children shall have freely . . . provided for them, at the . . . Company's charge . . . a house ready built to dwell in, and be placed as a tenant . . . upon so much land as they can manage. . . .

Moreover, that . . . the said children . . . which shall have thus served their apprenticeships . . . shall be tied to be tenants or farmers . . . for the space of seven years after their apprenticeships ended, and during that time, . . . they shall have half of all the . . . profit . . . and the other [profit] to go . . . to the owners of the land, . . . and that at the expiration of the . . . last seven years . . . the children [are] to be at liberty either to continue [as] tenants or farmers of the Company . . . or else provide for themselves elsewhere."

con's name, celebrated by the people in verse and song, would be invoked often in 1776 by the leaders of the American Revolution.

VIRGINIA AT THE END OF THE CENTURY

By the end of the seventeenth century, doubt no longer existed as to whether Virginia would survive as a colony. Virginia's population was seventy thousand, and its settlers continued to push farther into the frontier. Representative government was well established through the House of Burgesses, now firmly entrenched as a colonial institution.

Other colonies would suffer initial hardships, but none like Virginia. The first of the thirteen colonies paved the way for the other twelve, and it would continue to do so. It would be a Virginian who would stand before the Continental Congress in 1776 and call for independence from England.

3 Pilgrims and Puritans: Plymouth and Massachusetts

Religion played only a small role in the settlement of Virginia, but in Massachusetts it was a crucial factor. The founding of Massachusetts grew out of a dissatisfaction with religious conditions in England.

At the beginning of the seventeenth century, England was officially Protestant. The majority of the people belonged to the state church—the Church of England. But certain members were troubled that the church retained traces of Catholicism. These people, who became known as Puritans, wanted to purify the church by doing away with rituals and church hierarchy—priests and bishops.

Within the larger Puritan group was a segment of believers called Separatists. They wanted to separate from the Church of England and establish their own church. This did not set well with James I, who, as king, was head of the Church of England. He had some of the Separatists jailed and vowed to "harry them out of the land, or else do worse."[22] In 1608 they fled England for Holland.

In Holland the Pilgrims, as the Separatists came to be called, could worship as they pleased. But they were not happy to have their children growing up in a for-

eign country, speaking Dutch, and forgetting the English language and customs. Most of them were farmers who disliked living in the city. They wanted land of their own. And although they did not want to return to England itself, they wanted to live under the English flag. A further concern was that Catholic Spain might reconquer Holland and force the Catholic religion on them. So after twelve years in Holland, the Pilgrims decided to "dislodge . . . to some place of better advantage and less danger."[23] Where better than the New World?

SAINTS AND STRANGERS

The Pilgrims had no money to buy and equip a ship, so they formed a joint-stock company with some London businessmen. The merchants agreed to finance the venture in exchange for half of all profits generated in the first seven years. Although the Virginia Company granted the Pilgrims a patent that allowed them to settle in Virginia, the Pilgrims were not employees of a company as the Jamestown settlers had been; the Pilgrims were partners with the merchants.

Although King James refused to give the Pilgrims a charter, he promised that if they returned to England to embark on their journey, he "would not molest them, provided they carried themselves peaceably."[24] In September 1620 the Pilgrims boarded the *Mayflower* and set sail from Plymouth, England, with 101 passengers. Only 51 of the men, women, and children aboard were "Saints"—the name the Pilgrims called themselves; the others were of different faiths, and the Pilgrims called them "Strangers."

THE MAYFLOWER COMPACT

After sixty-five days at sea, the Pilgrims—either by accident or by intent—landed in New England instead of Virginia. They had no legal right to settle there because it was outside of their patent's jurisdiction.

When the Strangers realized they had not reached their promised destination, they thought they had been tricked and threatened mutiny.

The Pilgrim leaders moved quickly to quell this rebellion and establish some form of government until their settlement could be authorized by the king. They assembled all the men who were aboard ship and drew up the Mayflower Compact. This document was an early indication of the self-governing spirit that would drive the English colonists who settled America. In it they agreed to obey majority rule in the colony. However, they were careful to include a pledge of loyalty to King James:

> We . . . the loyal subjects of our dread sovereign lord, King James . . . having undertaken, for the glory of God, and advancement of the Christian faith . . .

The Mayflower Compact was one of the first examples of self-government among the English colonists.

a voyage to plant the first colony in the northern parts of Virginia, do . . . combine ourselves together into a civil body politic . . . to enact, constitute, and frame such just and equal laws . . . as shall be thought most meet [proper] and convenient for the general good of the colony, unto which we promise all due submission and obedience.[25]

Of the sixty-five adult male passengers, forty-one—Strangers as well as Saints—signed the agreement that would become Plymouth's constitution.

HARD TIMES AND GOOD FRIENDS

Landing on the New England coast in the middle of winter proved costly. Freezing weather and disease soon took its toll. By the end of winter, half of the Plymouth settlers had died.

Fortunately, the Pilgrims enjoyed a peaceful relationship with the Native Americans. This was partly because the local tribe had been too ravaged and weakened by smallpox to pose a threat. But it was also due to an Indian named Squanto. Years before the Pilgrims arrived, Squanto had been kidnapped by a passing English ship and sold into slavery in Spain. He had eventually made his way back to New England. Squanto spoke broken English and served as an interpreter for the Pilgrims. He also taught them how to plant corn, catch fish, and trap beaver. Squanto played an important part in the little colony's early survival.

The colony at Plymouth became self-supporting, and the Pilgrims lived peacefully alongside the Indians for forty years, but Plymouth remained a simple agricultural society small in number. The brave little band of Pilgrims who succeeded in carving out a tiny foothold on the wild and rugged New England coast never obtained a charter of their own.

Consequently, Plymouth eventually ceased being a separate colony. It was swallowed up by a more powerful and successful neighbor. For in 1630, the first of the enterprising Puritans arrived from England to establish the Massachusetts Bay Colony.

MIGRATING PURITANS

The Puritans had tried to reform the Church of England. When it became clear that the reforms were not going to happen, they resolved to establish a holy community in the midst of the New England wilderness, where the lives of individuals would be regulated in harmony with the will of God. But the Puritans were practical people. They wanted to make sure that they had a clear title to land in New England. That required obtaining a royal charter from Charles I, the reigning king. This seemed an impossible task because Charles—who was married to a French Catholic—despised the Puritans. Nevertheless, influential Puritans in Parliament persuaded him to grant a charter that formed twenty-six investors into the Massachusetts Bay Company. The company and the colony were synonymous until 1684.

THE WILDERNESS EXPERIENCE

William Bradford served as Plymouth's governor for over thirty years. In his history "Of Plimoth Plantation," he described the dangers Plymouth Pilgrims encountered when they arrived in New England. These excerpts are from U.S. Colonial History: Readings and Documents, *edited by David Hawke.*

William Bradford, governor of the Plymouth colony.

"Being thus arrived in a good harbor and brought safe to land, they fell upon their knees and blessed the God of heaven, who had brought them over the vast and furious ocean and delivered them from all the perils and miseries thereof. . . . Being thus passed the vast ocean, and a sea of troubles before . . . their [departure], . . . they had now no friends to welcome them nor inns to entertain or refresh their weather-beaten bodies; no houses or much less towns to repair to, to seek for succor [aid]. And . . . it was winter. . . . Besides, what could they see but a hideous and desolate wilderness, full of wild beasts and wild men?—and what multitudes there might be of them they knew not. . . . If they looked behind them, there was the mighty ocean [over] which they had passed and was now . . . a . . . gulf to separate them from all the civil parts of the world. . . . What could now sustain them but the spirit of God and his Grace? Ought not the children of these fathers rightly say: 'Our fathers were Englishmen which came over this great ocean and were ready to perish in this wilderness but they cried unto the Lord, and He heard their voice.'"

John Winthrop was a devout Puritan and the first governor of the Massachusetts Bay Colony.

America. The "Great Migration" had begun. Some 20,000 men and women would follow before the decade passed.

Unlike the Pilgrims, who came primarily from England's lower working classes, the Puritans represented all levels of English society. They included gentlemen of substantial means like Winthrop as well as merchants and lawyers, tradesmen and craftsmen, and a substantial number of yeoman farmers. But the "lesser sort," tenant farmers, unskilled workers, and servants, also joined the Puritan movement.

In June the Puritans got their first glimpse of New England, but before they saw it, they inhaled its aroma. "There came a smell off the shore like the smell of a garden,"[27] one wrote. They settled along Massachusetts Bay. A small number of Puritan and non-Puritan settlers were already scattered up and down the New England coast, and Winthrop began the process of governing approximately one thousand people. The Puritans would establish seven towns that first year, including Boston.

The migrating Puritans elected John Winthrop governor of the Massachusetts colony. Winthrop, a devout Puritan and an influential man in England, shared his fellow Puritans' vision of what could be accomplished in a "new" England. "We shall be like a City upon a Hill; the eyes of all people are on us,"[26] he wrote.

THE GREAT MIGRATION

Late in April 1630 eleven ships—carrying more than 700 men, women, and children; 240 cows; and 60 horses—embarked for

THE MASSACHUSETTS BAY GOVERNMENT

The terms of the Massachusetts charter put control of the colony into the hands of the governor, a deputy governor, and the seven freemen (members of the corporation) who migrated. They were authorized "to make . . . all manner of wholesome and reasonable . . . statutes"[28] for the colony.

However, government of the Massachusetts Bay Colony could not be left in the hands of so few. Membership in the corporation was soon expanded to include other adult males. Being a member meant having the right to vote in the General Court, Massachusetts's representative legislature. A member of the General Court was called a "freeman," and the word soon became synonymous with "voting citizen."

The number of freemen was limited, however, by the General Court's ruling that "noe man shal be admitted to the freedom of this body politicke, but such as are members of some of the [Puritan] churches."[29] This violated the charter, but for over fifty years no Massachusetts resident could vote in provincial elections unless he belonged to an accepted Puritan church. (Women were not allowed to vote under any circumstances.) But in an important step toward future separation of church and state, the Puritans barred ministers from holding political office.

REPRESENTATIVE GOVERNMENT GROWS

By 1634 Massachusetts contained three to four thousand inhabitants distributed over sixteen towns. No one would have called its government a democracy, but that year the freemen in each town gained the right to elect two representatives annually.

Soon, however, the colony's leaders grew fearful that the number of elected representatives would become large enough to control the vote. As a result,

---

"A CIVIL RIGHT"

John Winthrop wrote a paper before leaving England to answer the objections of Puritans who resisted immigrating. Some Puritans argued that they had no right to settle in a land that had long been possessed by others. Editor David Hawke includes Winthrop's arguments in U.S. Colonial History: Readings and Documents.

"That which lies common and hath never been replenished or subdued is free to any that will possess and improve it, for God hath given to . . . men a double right to the earth. There is a natural right and a civil right. The first right was natural when men held the earth in common. . . . And then as men and the cattle increased, they [claimed] certain parcels of ground by enclosing and peculiar manurance [occupancy]. And this in time gave them a civil right. . . . And for the natives in New England; they enclose no land, neither have any settled habitation, nor any tame cattle to improve the land by, and so have no other but a natural right to those countries. So . . . if we leave them [enough] for their use we may lawfully take the rest, there being more than enough for them and us."

the General Court split into two houses. The upper house consisted of the governor and his assistants and the lower house of the elected representatives. Any proposed law had to pass both houses. The General Court still allowed only male church members to vote, but the town meeting was becoming more and more popular. And at town meetings, all men could vote.

SEEDS OF COLONIAL UNITY

By 1640 New England included settlements in Rhode Island, Connecticut, New Hampshire, and Maine. The settlers had lived more or less peacefully with the Native Americans until the Pequot War in 1637—the first major struggle between the two cultures. That war, in which Massachusetts and Connecticut colonists all but eradicated the Pequot tribe, led to the formation of the New England Confederation. The confederation comprised Massachusetts, Plymouth, Connecticut, and New Haven. (Rhode Island was excluded because of the nonconformists there, and New Hampshire and Maine because they had no unified government.)

The purpose of the confederation was to defend the colonies against the Indians and from possible outside invasion by the French and the Dutch. (The colonists

The war against the Pequot tribe in 1637 laid the foundation for future colonial unity.

could not depend on the mother country to help them because England was embroiled in a civil war.) The confederation read in part,

> We live encompassed with people of several nations and strange languages which . . . have of late combined themselves against us; and seeing . . . we are hindered from . . . seeking advice, or protection [from England] . . . do conceive it our bounded duty . . . to enter into a . . . consociation [alliance] among ourselves, for mutual help and strength.[30]

This confederation was the earliest sign of the colonial unity that would develop in the next century.

MASSACHUSETTS REACTS TO CIVIL WAR IN ENGLAND

Meanwhile, England in 1640 was divided by a civil war that would lead to the overthrow and beheading of Charles I. In 1649 Oliver Cromwell and the Puritans took over England's government.

Massachusetts was quick to take advantage of the disarray in England. The colony had always exhibited an unusual independence. Now with the mother country distracted, Massachusetts began coining its own money, creating corporations, and establishing its own commercial system—none of which it had a legal right to do. The day of reckoning came in 1660 with the restoration of the monarchy. Charles II took a renewed and critical interest in Massachusetts.

MASSACHUSETTS LOSES ITS CHARTER

King Charles II not only extended the Navigation Acts that regulated colonial trade, he was also determined to enforce them. Massachusetts colonists, by now bent on governing themselves, responded arrogantly to the monarch's efforts. In words that anticipated colonial America's rebellion a century later, the Massachusetts General Court informed England,

> Wee humbly conceive that the lawes of England are bounded within the four seas, and doe not reach America. The subjects of his majesty here being not represented in Parliament, so we have not looked at ourselves to be impeded in our trade by them.[31]

The king at first ignored this insolence, but in 1675 he sent his agent, Edward Randolph, to investigate conditions in the colony. Randolph found Massachusetts guilty of religious intolerance, of openly violating the Navigation Acts, and of repeatedly exceeding the limitations imposed by its charter. On the basis of Randolph's report, the crown revoked Massachusetts's charter in 1684. This was a harsh blow for a people who revered their charter, but it was only the first of more to come.

THE DOMINION OF NEW ENGLAND

One year after the Massachusetts charter was annulled, James II succeeded his

KING PHILIP'S WAR

The same year that Massachusetts lost its charter, the colony suffered a devastating Indian attack. Twelve towns were destroyed and six hundred colonists killed. The following description of what was called King Philip's War is from The Search for Liberty by Esmond Wright.

"[Chief] Massasoit's death . . . brought an end to the era of good relations between the Massachusetts colonists and the Wampanoags. He had faithfully kept the peace for 40 years, since signing the treaty of 1621 with the Pilgrims. Numerous injustices, many having their roots in quarrels over land sales to the expanding settlements, were visited on the Indians, and in 1675 the largest and bloodiest Indian war broke out and spread quickly across eastern Massachusetts and Rhode Island. The new Wampanoag leader, Metacomet, a son of Massasoit known to the English as King Philip, was proud, statesmanlike, and courageous. . . . His initial successes induced other tribes . . . to join him in a tribal confederation stretching from Maine to Connecticut. The Indian allies enjoyed dramatic victories, attacking 52 of the 90 white settlements in the then West, claiming that they had never granted the land away permanently, but only the use. . . . Then the tide turned. The Indians . . . began to run out of food. Philip suffered serious defections; and defeatist Indians began to help the colonists track down the warriors. The Narragansetts were caught in a swamp and suffered a crippling defeat, and with the help of an Indian informer Philip himself was found and killed, and his body quartered and exposed; the individual warring bands of Wampanoags and Nipmucks were wiped out one by one. . . . The natives' power came to an end in New England in 1676. Nevertheless, this . . . frontier war inflicted greater casualties in proportion to population than any other war in American history."

Wampanoag chief, Metacomet, also known as King Philip, led a futile attempt to drive English settlers from Indian lands.

brother Charles as king. James consolidated the New England colonies, along with New York and New Jersey, into a single unit called the Dominion of New England. He appointed Sir Edmund Andros royal governor over the dominion.

The dominion's bylaws made no provision for a representative assembly, and Andros was given dictatorial powers. He enraged the Puritans by flaunting his Church of England beliefs and by questioning the validity of all New England land titles. He also enforced the Navigation Acts, which controlled colonial trade, to the letter of the law. Those accused of violations were tried by judges expert in maritime law rather than by a jury. Everything the Puritans held dear—representative government, landownership, and trial by jury—was in jeopardy. However, in England a revolution was brewing against the king.

Bostonians celebrate the resignation of Sir Edmund Andros after the Glorious Revolution of 1688.

THE GLORIOUS REVOLUTION

In 1688 England forced James II to flee the country during what became known as the Glorious Revolution because it was accomplished without bloodshed. The result was an English Bill of Rights that gave Parliament (and thus the people) more power than the monarchy.

When news of the Glorious Revolution reached Boston on April 4, 1689, the Bostonians staged their own revolution. They called a town meeting, dissolved the Dominion government, and forced the despised Andros to resign.

The Glorious Revolution ended the Dominion of New England, but it did not restore all of the old ways. In 1691 the king made Massachusetts a royal colony. The colony was allowed to keep its popularly elected lower house of the General Court, but voting rights—previously open only to church members—were extended to all qualified male property holders. They could not elect a governor, however, because the governor would now be appointed by the Crown. Puritan political leadership in Massachusetts had been declining since 1660. Church membership had decreased, and political power was moving into the hands of the merchants,

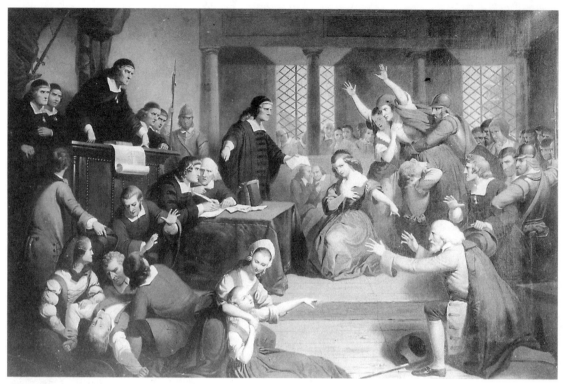

Support of the Salem witch trials led to the decline of Puritan influence in Massachusetts's colonial government.

who increasingly controlled the colony's economy. The king's changes served to further weaken Puritan control.

What little power or influence the Puritans did retain was lost when Puritan ministers supported an outbreak of witch-hunts that occurred in Salem from 1692 to 1693. The witch hysteria began when certain young girls in the town accused several older women of being witches. Before it ended, 20 "witches" were executed, and 150 more were jailed.

The Puritan ministers' loss of respect and prestige that resulted from their support of the Salem witch trials dealt the final blow to the Puritan ruling class. The orthodox Puritans never regained their previous hold on Massachusetts government, but the Puritan ideals—their courage and willingness to sacrifice for their beliefs, their dedication to individual freedom—lived on in generations of Americans. Historian Page Smith writes that the Puritans "determined the character . . . of [the] New World more . . . than any other body of people who came to the English colonies."[32] Massachusetts, in particular, would demonstrate that heritage during colonial America's fight for independence in the eighteenth century.

4 Puritan Offshoots: Rhode Island, Connecticut, and New Hampshire

Rhode Island, Connecticut, and New Hampshire were settled by emigrants from Massachusetts. Much of this hiving off resulted from the never-ending search for more fertile land. Another driving force was disagreement over religious issues. Many nonconformists, who differed with Massachusetts authorities over biblical interpretations, left of their own accord. But some—like Roger Williams, the founder of Rhode Island—were forced to leave.

A CHARMING REBEL

Roger Williams was an outspoken, opinionated, and stubborn man, but he had a charismatic charm that attracted followers. In the eyes of the Massachusetts government, this made Williams a danger. He first got into trouble when he publicly declared that the Massachusetts Bay Colony had no legal title to its land. He said the land still belonged to the Indians because no one had paid them for it.

Roger Williams was banished from Massachusetts and eventually founded a colony in Rhode Island.

Then, in 1635, when Williams had been in the colony four years, Massachusetts passed a law that made church attendance mandatory and imposed a tax that would be used to support the church. Williams openly opposed both measures on the grounds that government should not interfere in religious matters. This time Williams had gone too far. He was tried in the General Court and was banished from the colony.

In the dead of winter, Williams trudged across the frozen countryside until he reached a Wampanoag village on Narragansett Bay, located just outside the jurisdiction of Massachusetts. He had earlier forged a friendly relationship with the Wampanoag and had learned some of their language. The tribe members welcomed Williams, and he remained with them until the spring.

Providence

In June Williams bought land from the Indians and, along with a number of other Massachusetts outcasts, established the town of Providence. Like the Plymouth Pilgrims, they created a government for themselves by signing a compact. In it they agreed to "subject ourselves in active and passive obedience to all such orders and agreements as shall be made . . . by the major consent of the present inhabitants . . . and others whom they shall hereafter admit unto them, [but] only in civil things."[33] The document was remarkable for its time because it limited the power of civil government, recognized the principle of major-

ity rule, and endorsed separation of church and state. The right to vote was limited to property owners, but it did not depend on church membership as in Massachusetts.

Rhode Island Grows

Other Massachusetts rebels sought refuge in Rhode Island—people like the exiled religious leader Anne Hutchinson and Samuel Gorton, an eccentric, cantankerous intellectual who had "developed a theology that was peculiar to himself."[34] These outcasts added three more towns: Portsmouth, Newport, and Warwick.

However, Rhode Island's four towns were, for all practical purposes, four independent governments; no unity or cooperation existed among them. And Rhode Islanders lived in fear of being taken over by the stronger New England colonies that considered Rhode Island "the sink of New England."[35] Roger Williams, already troubled by his colony's lack of unity, became doubly concerned when these neighboring colonies excluded Rhode Island from their newly formed New England Confederation.

Rhode Island Gets a Charter

Rhode Island needed a charter from the king that would ensure legal title to its land, and Roger Williams hurried off to England to obtain one. Despite a strong Massachusetts attempt to sabotage his efforts, Williams returned with a charter dated March 24, 1644, that made Rhode Island an official colony and united the towns.

Disagreeing with church officials over accepted Puritan thinking, Anne Hutchinson was banished from Massachusetts and settled in Rhode Island.

government, Rhode Islanders worried that the restored king would not accept it as a legal charter. He might even break up their colony and divide it among the other New England colonies. They decided to petition the king for a new charter. In 1663 Charles II granted the charter, and Rhode Islanders breathed a collective sigh of relief. One provision that was added to the charter (probably at Williams's insistence) made it different from any charter ever issued by the monarchy. It stipulated that

> no person within the colonie at any time hereafter, shall be anywise molested, punished, disquieted, or called in question, for any difference in

King Charles II granted the charter that saved Rhode Island and allowed religious freedom in the colony.

Securing a charter did not solve all of Rhode Island's problems, though. Years of bitter wrangling over land claims followed. Nevertheless, Williams managed to keep Rhode Island united, even when the New England Confederation—angry that Rhode Island welcomed dissenting religious groups like the Quakers—threatened to cut off trade and reduce the tiny colony to bankruptcy. Then, in 1660, the restoration of the monarchy in England appeared to jeopardize the colony's survival.

A NEW AND MOST UNUSUAL CHARTER

Because Rhode Island's charter had been granted under the Puritan Commonwealth opinions in matters of religion . . . but may . . . at all tymes hereafter, freelye and fullye have and enjoy his and their owne judgements and consciences, in matters of religious concernments.[36]

The colony founded by fugitives and exiles would remain a place where people could dare to be different.

CONNECTICUT: CONFORMING PURITANS

Unlike Rhode Island, Connecticut was founded by strictly orthodox Puritans who were attracted by Connecticut's rich, fertile farmlands—a striking contrast to the thin, rocky soil of Massachusetts. The colony had its beginnings in 1633 when John Oldham, a fur trader in search of

THE FIRST MIGRANT FROM BOSTON TO RHODE ISLAND

The first settler in Boston was an Anglican, not a Puritan. Historian Esmond Wright describes this early pioneer in The Search for Liberty.

"The rebel Anglican churchman, Reverend William Blaxton or Blackstone . . . sought solitude with his 180 books in a house on Beacon Hill, with an orchard below him on the Common. The first settler in what would become Boston, he developed the first named variety of apple in America, 'Blaxton's Yellow Sweeting.' The first Bostonian was also its first eccentric: when not tending his orchard, he rode about the three-hilled peninsula on a saddled bull he had trained. When the Puritans reached Charlestown and wanted—as ever—to expand across the river to the more inviting prospect of what the Indians called the Shawmut peninsula, with its three hills promising freedom from mosquitoes, they promised him [Blaxton] 50 acres. This was, it seemed, no bargain for him, since it had all been his anyway. . . . But the eccentric had a shrewdness all his own. He accepted their generosity, and then sold them back their 50 acres for $150, a princely sum for what, after all, was not originally his at all. In England, he said, he didn't like the Lords Bishops; he would not now be under the Lords Brethren. He preferred Indians, and rum, he said, to Puritans, who did not like either. So he uprooted himself and moved to Rhode Island, where he lived in happy isolation, with only books, rum and Indians for solace, until he was 80."

Thomas Hooker leads a group of settlers from Massachusetts to Connecticut.

beaver pelts, followed ancient Indian trails overland from Massachusetts to the Connecticut River. Two years later he and a small group of settlers established the town of Wethersfield. Oldham opened the floodgates for a westward migration of Massachusetts farmers seeking good farmland.

THOMAS HOOKER

One Massachusetts settler eager to join the Connecticut migration was the Reverend Thomas Hooker. Harassed out of England because of his Puritan sentiments, he had arrived in Boston in 1633 accompanied by his congregation. Hooker was not a radical like Roger Williams, but he did believe that Massachusetts's religious qualifications for voting placed government in the hands of too few people. He thought issues that affected everyone should be decided by "a general counsel chosen by all."[37]

In September 1634 Hooker sought authorization from the Massachusetts General Court to settle in Connecticut. The General Court initially denied permission on the grounds that "the departure of Mr. Hooker would not only draw many from us, but [would] also divert other friends that would come to us."[38] However, when a scattering of people began leaving despite the ruling, the court reversed its decision with the understanding that the Connecticut immigrants would still be governed by Massachusetts. The General Court appointed an eight-man commission—all of whom were in Connecticut or were preparing to go there—to govern for one year. Hooker and his followers were free to go.

WESTWARD HO!

On May 31, 1636, thirty-five men with wives, children, servants, and cattle headed west, following one of the Indian paths. It took nearly two weeks, traveling on foot and sleeping under the trees at night, before they reached the settlement that would become the town of Hartford.

Approximately eight hundred people were scattered along the Connecticut River in three separate towns: Wethersfield, Windsor, and Hartford. When the term of the Massachusetts-appointed commission ended in May 1637, the three towns immediately organized themselves into the self-governing colony of Connecticut. There was no time to waste because war with the Pequot tribe was at hand. Wethersfield had already been attacked.

THE PEQUOT MASSACRE

The Pequot tribe had migrated into Connecticut and settled near the Mystic River. As more English settlers moved into the Connecticut Valley, the Pequot grew increasingly aggressive. In 1633 the tribe had wiped out a small band of English traders near the mouth of the Connecticut River. A year later, when the Pequot murdered trader John Oldham, Massachusetts sent a force of one hundred men in retaliation. They plundered the Pequot villages and burned their crops, intensifying the tribe's anger.

The Pequot tribe continued to ravage the Connecticut countryside. In the spring of 1637, the Connecticut towns sent ninety men led by John Mason to confront the Indians in their fort at Mystic. After convincing the Pequot that he did not want to fight, Mason led his men in a surprise night attack on the unsuspecting Indians. The men set fire to the fort, and those Indians who were not burned to death were shot down as they ran screaming from the fort. Colonist William Bradford chronicled the massacre:

> It was a fearfull sight . . . to see them thus frying in the fyer [fire], and the streams of blood quenching the same, and horrible was the stinck and sente [scent] ther of, but the victory seemed a sweete sacrifice, and they gave the prays there of to God . . . who had give them so speedy a victory over so proud and insulting an enimie.[39]

Of the four hundred men, women, and children in the fort, all but five were killed. Massachusetts sent reinforcements, and the remaining members of the Pequot tribe were hunted down and virtually exterminated. Mason wrote in his account: "Thus, the LORD was pleased to smite our Enemies . . . and to give us their land for an Inheritance."[40]

THE FUNDAMENTAL ORDERS

After the Pequot crisis, Connecticut turned to matters of government. In 1639, guided by Thomas Hooker, the General Court created a body of laws called the Fundamental Orders of Connecticut.

The Fundamental Orders became the colony's constitution. The document foreshadowed the U.S. Constitution because it sounded a new note in government. "The foundation of all authority is laid . . . in the free consent of the people."[41] On paper, the right to vote was not to be based on any religious affiliation; however, in actual practice, it was mostly limited to those who were of an "approved" religion. Nonetheless, the concept of democratic government had been expressed. Meanwhile, a new colony that formed at the mouth of the Quinnipiac River in southern Connecticut had a different understanding of government.

THE NEW HAVEN COLONY

John Davenport, a nonconformist pastor who had fled persecution in England, established New Haven in March 1638. New Haven's government was stricter than in other Puritan colonies—even in Massachusetts. The "New Haven Way"

Led by Captain John Mason, settlers from Connecticut killed four hundred men, women, and children of the Pequot tribe.

THE FUNDAMENTAL ORDERS OF CONNECTICUT

The Fundamental Orders expressed the belief that government should abide in the free consent of the people. But historian Charles M. Andrews explains in The Colonial Period of American History *that putting this belief into practice depended on the definition of "consent of the people."*

"This matter of the franchise [right to vote] at the beginnings of Connecticut's history has been greatly misunderstood. . . . It has been assumed that every male adult in the colony was given a right to a share in government and that in the exercise of that right the majority ruled. Nothing could be farther from the truth. The Fundamental Orders . . . make a sharp distinction between one who voted in the town and one who voted for colony officers, that is, between an 'admitted inhabitant' and a 'freeman. . . .' An 'admitted inhabitant'. . . could take part in local affairs, join in the election of local officials, and vote for deputies to the general court. But being an 'admitted inhabitant' did not make a man a 'freeman.' The [freeman] was any 'admitted inhabitant' who had been selected for freemanship . . . by the general court. . . . Only when thus admitted to freemanship could the adult male householder offer himself for election as a deputy, vote for the higher officials of the colony and himself fill the post of magistrate [on the General Court]. . . . As neither women, servants, apprentices, nor anyone convicted of a scandalous offense were allowed to exercise the franchise or to have any part in the government of town or colony, it happened from the beginning that in the actual working out of the system the words 'people' and 'inhabitants' acquired a meaning much more restricted than that commonly given to them today."

Even though the Fundamental Orders of Connecticut expanded voting rights, defining who was an "approved" voter still proved difficult.

The New Haven colony, founded by John Davenport, followed a much stricter code than the other New England colonies.

decreed that "the Word of God shall be the only rule to be attended unto in ordering the affairs of government in this plantation."[42] Trial by jury, for example, was dispensed with because it was not found in the Mosaic law.

Throughout New Haven's existence, its inhabitants battled to remain an independent colony. But in 1662 the king ordered New Haven to unite with Connecticut.

THE CONNECTICUT CHARTER

Connecticut had originated without a charter and therefore had no legal claim to its land. After the restoration of the monarchy in England, Connecticut sent its governor, John Winthrop Jr., to obtain a royal charter from Charles II.

Winthrop's assignment was a difficult one. Puritans had been responsible for the beheading of Charles I, the new king's father. How Winthrop managed to secure a charter for a Puritan colony under these circumstances remains a mystery. But in 1662 Charles II issued an unusually liberal charter—based on the Fundamental Orders—that made Connecticut a royal colony.

When the Dominion of New England was formed and Sir Edmund Andros demanded the surrender of all charters, Connecticut refused. Legend has it that the inhabitants hid it in a great oak tree that later came to be called the Charter Oak. After the Glorious Revolution of 1688 ended the dominion, Connecticut quietly resumed its old government and entered the eighteenth century with its charter intact.

New Hampshire: The Last New England Colony

New Hampshire's beginning was unlike that of any other New England colony. It did not even become a colony until 1679. Instead, for nearly a century its early settlers struggled with internal discord, landownership squabbles, and conflicting sentiments toward nearby acquisitive Massachusetts.

New Hampshire's story began in 1620 when James I established the Council of New England, a joint-stock company made up of wealthy English noblemen. Two members who received a large grant of land in New England were Sir Ferdinando Gorges and Captain John Mason (not the John Mason who led the attack on the Pequot tribe).

Mason and Gorges formed the Laconia Company and sent two small groups of settlers to New England. Although they spent large sums of money to keep the settlements well supplied, the fur trade they envisioned failed to materialize. The Laconia Company folded in 1634, and Mason and Gorges divided their holdings. Mason took the land south of the Piscataqua River and named it New Hampshire after Hampshire County in England. Gorges took the territory north of the river that would become Maine. Mason continued to provide New Hampshire with supplies and financial support until his death in December 1635.

Massachusetts Residents Migrate to New Hampshire

Most Puritans had stayed clear of New Hampshire because its founders and settlers supported the Church of England. But after Mason's death a steady stream of colonists migrated from Massachusetts, and by 1640 the two Puritan towns of Exeter and Hampton had been established.

Hampton—settled by orthodox Puritans from Massachusetts—chose to remain under that colony's jurisdiction. But Exeter—founded by Puritan minister John Wheelwright, who had been banished from Massachusetts for his religious beliefs—managed to remain independent of Massachusetts for three years.

Joining Massachusetts

Uncompromising religious differences prevented the four New Hampshire towns from uniting, yet the towns were not strong enough to stand alone. In 1641 they asked Massachusetts for help. Massachusetts pounced on the opportunity to establish control over the New Hampshire towns.

In an often uneasy relationship, New Hampshire remained under Massachusetts authority for almost forty years. With England distracted by civil war,

FRENCH AND INDIAN WARFARE IN NEW HAMPSHIRE

After becoming a royal colony in 1679, New Hampshire was involved in frontier warfare for nearly a quarter of a century. Jere R. Daniell describes these tumultuous years in his book, Colonial New Hampshire.

"Indian attacks against settlements in Dover during the summer of 1689 were the initial skirmishes of frontier warfare.... The costs of war were immense: Eastern Indians and their French allies either killed or captured hundreds of inhabitants, the economy stagnated, and daily life in many parts of the colony was shaped by the constant fear of sudden assault....

In a formal sense the conflict was two separate wars. The first, known ... in the colonies ... as King William's War, began in 1688.... New Hampshire was in constant danger throughout King William's War. In March 1690 ... a combined force of French and Indians destroyed the settlement at Salmon Falls, only a few miles up the Newichiwannock from Great Bay. That summer more than thirty inhabitants lost their lives when Indians attacked in and around Exeter. After a short truce the raids began again. Between 1692 and 1696 Portsmouth was invaded four separate times with heavy loss of life; the various settlements in Dover fared even worse. Exeter and Hampton experienced less difficulty but were constantly alerted by reports of marauding Indians in the vicinity....

The second phase of intercolonial fighting, Queen Anne's War, began in 1703.... New Hampshire was now better prepared.... They could not, however, protect the frontier completely.... The raids continued until 1713.... That summer the exhausted leaders of both English and Native American nations met in Portsmouth to sign a separate peace treaty."

For much of its early colonial history, New Hampshire was involved in wars with Indian tribes.

Many of New Hampshire's early settlers were colonists from Massachusetts.

the powerful colony of Massachusetts—claiming ownership under its charter—increasingly encroached on New Hampshire territory. John Mason's heirs protested, but because they were known to support the dethroned monarchy, they could do nothing. Once the monarchy was restored, they appealed to Charles II; in January 1680 the king declared New Hampshire a royal colony separate from Massachusetts.

Royal Governor Edward Cranfield

At the outset, no royal governor was sent to New Hampshire. In 1682, however, Edward Cranfield, "a royal governor whose behavior alienated virtually everyone,"[43] arrived.

New Hampshire residents resented the royal authority of a "crew of pitiful curs . . . come to undo us both body and soul."[44]

They resisted in ways that ranged from generally making Cranfield's life miserable to staging a small armed uprising. After little more than a year, Cranfield requested a new assignment. When it was granted, he wrote to the king's council in England: "I esteem it the greatest happiness that ever I had in my life that your Lordships have given me an opportunity to remove from these unreasonable people. . . . No man shall be acceptable to them that puts his Majesty's commands in execution."[45]

More Turmoil

As in other colonies, the Dominion of New England temporarily replaced New Hampshire's government. After the dominion's collapse, the colony attempted to draw up a new plan of government, but the towns could not agree on its form. Without a unified government, New

Hampshire was vulnerable to attack from French Canadians and their Native American allies. Rejoining Massachusetts appeared to be the only choice. A petition was drawn up asking Massachusetts for temporary annexation, and in 1690 New Hampshire once again became a part of Massachusetts.

ROYAL STATUS RESUMED

Massachusetts hoped to make the annexation of New Hampshire permanent; however, England's new monarchs, William and Mary, were intent on bringing Massachusetts into line. In 1692 New Hampshire was reestablished as a royal colony.

The years ahead would not be easy for New Hampshire. Bloody frontier wars with the Native Americans began in 1689 and lasted well into the eighteenth century. Likewise, boundary disputes with Massachusetts continued, and a parade of royal officials came and went. But gradually the quarreling lessened, and the people united in a common goal to ensure New Hampshire's survival as an independent colony.

5 Catholic Haven: Maryland

Maryland was a new experiment in colonizing. The prominent Calvert family founded the colony as a refuge for England's persecuted Roman Catholics. The family's patriarch, George Calvert, was an esteemed politician who served as secretary of state until he converted to Catholicism in 1625. This was an unpopular decision in a primarily Protestant country where Catholics were even more harassed than Puritans. Nevertheless, Calvert remained a favorite of King James, who made him a baron with the title Lord Baltimore.

In 1632 James's son Charles I granted Calvert 10 million acres of land on the Chesapeake Bay north of Virginia to "be called Mariland in memory and honor of the Queene."[46] George Calvert died before the grant became official, but it was issued to his son Cecilius, who became the second Lord Baltimore.

Maryland became the first enduring, privately owned colony in the New World. Unlike royal colonies that were ruled directly by the monarchy, a proprietary colony was ruled by the owner or proprietor. This was especially true in Lord Baltimore's case. His charter gave him absolute control over the administration, defense, and upkeep of his province. In return, he promised to give the Crown one-fifth of all gold and silver discovered in Maryland and to pay the symbolic tribute of two Indian arrowheads a year. He was free to make all laws as long as they were not contrary to those of England. One important restriction, however, was that he must have "the advice, assent, and approbation [approval] of the freemen [white male property owners]"[47] in the colony.

SETTLEMENT AT ST. MARYS

In November 1633 the first group of Maryland immigrants left England in two ships, the *Ark* and the *Dove.* On board were two Jesuit priests, seventeen Roman Catholic gentlemen with their wives, and approximately two hundred others, most of whom were Church of England Protestants. (Protestants were included because too few Catholics were willing to leave England.) Lord Baltimore, who remained in England to protect his interests, sent his brother Leonard Calvert to govern for him.

The *Ark* and the *Dove* arrived in Chesapeake Bay on February 23, 1634. The colonists selected a healthful site on a high bluff overlooking the bay for their first settlement and named it St. Marys. The well-governed community prospered from the beginning. Colonists balanced growing tobacco, their highly profitable export,

---

PROMOTING COLONIZATION IN MARYLAND

Andrew White, a Jesuit missionary, accompanied the first Maryland settlers. The following excerpts are from a pamphlet he wrote in 1633. Cecilius Calvert, the second Lord Baltimore, circulated the somewhat exaggerated commentary to encourage colonization. The tract is reprinted in The Mind and Spirit of Early America, *edited by Richard Walsh.*

"This province, his most serene majesty . . . in the month of June, 1632, gave to the Lord Baron of Baltimore and his heirs forever. . . . Therefore the . . . Baron has resolved immediately to lead a colony into that region. . . . He has . . . weighed . . . all the advantages and disadvantages which hitherto advanced or impeded other colonies, and found nothing which does not . . . promise . . . success. . . . Such gentlemen as shall pay down one hundred pounds . . . to convey five men . . . shall be assigned . . . two thousand acres of good land. . . .

The natural position of the [colony] is . . . advantageous. . . . The air is serene and mild, neither exposed to the burning heat of Florida or ancient Virginia, nor withered by the cold of New England, but . . . enjoys the advantages of each. . . . On the east it is washed by the ocean: on the west it adjoins an almost boundless continent. . . .

There are two . . . bays most abundant in fish . . . and noble rivers . . . where . . . trade with the Indians is so profitable that a certain merchant, the last year, shipped beaver skins at a price of forty thousand pieces of gold. . . . In the level . . . country, there is a great abundance of grass, but the region is for the most part shaded with forests; oaks and walnut trees are the most common. . . .

So great is the abundance of swine and deer that they are [more] troublesome than profitable. Cows, also, are innumerable. . . . What shall I say of the lupines, beans, garden roots . . . when even the peas . . . grow in ten days, to a height of fourteen inches. . . . There is hope, too, of finding gold; for the neighboring people wear bracelets of unwrought gold and long strings of pearls."

with growing corn for food, and they bartered with the local Yoacomaco Indians. As a result, Maryland suffered few of the hardships that had plagued Virginia.

GOVERNMENT AND SOCIAL STATUS

Lord Baltimore envisioned a colony based on the feudal system in England. He instructed his brother to set up manorial estates—large tracts of land called manors—and to lease them to nobles who would have tenants to work the land. Relatives of Lord Baltimore received six thousand acres, and "gentlemen" who brought with them five other people received two thousand. These manor lords, who were of the Catholic elite, in turn rented smaller plots to farmers and tenants called freeholders.

This unequal system of land grants within the colony created social and class distinctions. Financial success determined social standing and political power. And because most of the landed aristocracy were Roman Catholics, Catholics controlled the Maryland assembly. Soon, though, more people demanded a voice in the government.

In 1637 Lord Baltimore officially appointed his brother Leonard Calvert governor. Leonard dutifully called assemblies into session for their advice and consent, as stipulated by the charter. But he soon found that the assembly members wanted to do more than approve laws initiated by the proprietor—they wanted to draft laws of their own. To get legislation approved, Lord Baltimore would eventually be compelled to permit the assembly to initiate laws.

SIBLING RIVALRY

Maryland was the sister colony of nearby Virginia. And like sisters they shared com-

The first settlement in Maryland was at St. Mary's, and good relations with the Indians helped the colony avoid many of the hardships that plagued Jamestown.

Lord Baltimore's Instructions to the Immigrants

Lord Baltimore's instructions to the first group of immigrants to Maryland reflected his desire to avoid friction between the Protestants and the Roman Catholics. He also suggested ways to approach the trespasser William Claiborne and how to avoid problems with Virginia. The following excerpts are from editor David Hawke's U.S. Colonial History: Readings and Documents.

"His Lordship requires [of] his . . . governor and commissioners that in their voyage to Maryland they be very careful to preserve unity and peace among all the passengers on shipboard and that they suffer no . . . offense to be given to any of the Protestants . . . and that . . . all acts of Roman Catholic religion [are] to be done as privately as [possible] and that they instruct all the Roman Catholics to be silent upon all occasions of discourse concerning matters of religion; and that the said governor and commissioners treat the Protestants with as much mildness and favor as justice will permit. And this to be observed at land as well as at sea. . . .

That they write a letter to Captain [William] Claiborne . . . to invite him kindly to come unto them. . . . And that they assure him . . . that his lordship [Lord Baltimore] intends not to do him any wrong . . . in confidence that he will, like a good subject to his majesty, conform himself to his . . . highness's . . . patent granted to his lordship. . . .

That . . . they be very careful to do justice to every man without partiality and that they avoid any occasion of difference [disagreement] with those of Virginia and to have as little to do with them as they can this first year . . . rather than to engage themselves in a public quarrel with them."

mon traits. The economy of both depended on tobacco, and by the end of the seventeenth century, Maryland's political system would be identical to Virginia's. But in the early going, they also quarreled like sisters, mostly over the question of boundary lines. One such conflict involved William Claiborne's claim to Kent Island in Virginia.

Claiborne had purchased Kent Island when it was part of Virginia—before Lord Baltimore received his proprietorship. Baltimore was willing to acknowledge Claiborne's ownership of the property, but only if Claiborne would admit that the island was part of Maryland and was thus under Baltimore's control. Claiborne refused. He regarded Baltimore's claim as an intrusion on his individual rights. Also, as an ardent Protestant, he was unwilling to be governed by a Roman Catholic. The controversy led to a violent

William Claiborne's retake of Kent Island by military force was a point of contention in Maryland's early colonial history.

confrontation with bloodshed on both sides. Finally, in 1638 authorities in England stepped in and ruled that Kent Island did belong under the jurisdiction of Lord Baltimore, temporarily ending the quarrel.

ENGLAND'S CIVIL WAR DIVIDES MARYLAND

During England's 1642 civil war, Maryland Protestants became more aggressive toward their Catholic-controlled government. The possibility of Indian warfare also threatened, and by 1643 the situation had become so critical that Leonard Calvert traveled to England to consult with his brother.

William Claiborne chose this time to retake Kent Island by military force. St. Marys was also captured, and when the governor returned after a year in England, he was forced to seek refuge in Virginia. For two years Maryland's government was in turmoil until Calvert regained control.

THE TOLERATION ACT

By 1648 Puritans in Virginia were being persecuted as a result of the ongoing civil war in England. Virginians, most of whom were fiercely loyal to the king, resented the Puritans who supported the king's enemies. Consequently, four hundred to six hundred Puritans left Virginia that year for the more tolerant Maryland. Lord Baltimore welcomed them and even granted them land, but the Puritans soon took advantage of his generosity. By receiving the Puritans, Lord Baltimore opened the door to a group that would try to undo all that he had done to bring about religious tolerance.

Catholics had always held the important government offices in Maryland, even though the majority of Maryland colonists were Protestants. After the influx from Virginia, Catholics were further outnumbered—three to one. Therefore, in 1649, hoping to maintain religious peace, Lord Baltimore replaced the Catholic governor with a Protestant one.

That same year—partly to protect the Catholic minority from persecution and partly because he genuinely believed in religious tolerance—Baltimore passed the Toleration Act, guaranteeing religious freedom to all Christians. Although this law applied only to Christians, it was an important step toward religious forbearance in America.

LORD BALTIMORE IS DEPRIVED OF HIS GOVERNING POWERS

In spite of Lord Baltimore's efforts, the Puritan Commonwealth, which had replaced the monarchy in England, accused Maryland of disloyalty. In 1652 the Commonwealth sent commissioners to the colony to set up a Puritan government, causing civil war to erupt in Maryland.

LEONARD CALVERT PLANTING THE FIRST COLONY IN MARYLAND.

Maryland was originally founded as a refuge for England's persecuted Catholic population.

THE MARYLAND TOLERATION ACT

As Protestants increasingly outnumbered Catholics in Maryland, Lord Baltimore moved to protect the religious freedom of Catholics. In 1649 he passed the Toleration Act—a milestone in the history of religious freedom for Protestants as well as Catholics. The text of this progressive document is included in The Annals of America, *edited by Mortimer J. Adler.*

"Whereas the enforcing of the conscience in matters of religion has frequently fallen out to be of dangerous consequence in those commonwealths where it has been practiced, and for the more quiet and peaceable government of this province, and the better to preserve mutual love and amity among the inhabitants thereof, be it, therefore, also by the Lord Proprietary, with the advice and consent of this assembly, ordained and enacted . . . that no person or persons whatsoever within this province . . . professing to believe in Jesus Christ, shall from henceforth be in any way troubled, molested, or discountenanced for . . . his or her religion, nor in the free exercise thereof . . . nor in any way compelled to the belief or exercise of any other religion against his or her consent. . . .

And that all . . . that shall presume . . . willfully to wrong, disturb, trouble, or molest any person whatsoever within this province professing to believe in Jesus Christ for . . . his or her religion or the free exercise thereof . . . that such person or persons so offending shall be compelled to pay treble [triple] damages to the party so wronged or molested. . . . If the party so offending shall refuse or be unable to recompense the party so wronged, or to satisfy such fine or forfeiture, then such offender shall be severely punished by public whipping and imprisonment."

The victorious Puritans repealed the Toleration Act and enacted a new law declaring that "none who profess and exercise the Popish [Catholic] religion . . . can be protected in this province."[48] Lord Baltimore was deprived of his administrative powers but retained his property rights.

The Puritans, still not satisfied, wanted Lord Baltimore's entire proprietorship annulled.

In England, however, Baltimore managed to win the support of Oliver Cromwell, the leader of the Commonwealth government. Baltimore regained control of his colony in 1657 and reinstated the Toleration Act. "Baltimore," historian Charles M. Andrews writes, "[came] out of the long ordeal with increased rather than diminished influence."[49] Three years later Puritan rule in England was overthrown, the monarchy was restored, and Charles II was seated on the throne.

TENSIONS RISING

In 1661 Lord Baltimore appointed his son Charles Calvert governor of Maryland. He instructed him to continue calling general assemblies "for the giving of the advice, assent and approbation [approval] by the freemen to such laws and acts as shall be by us att any time ordayned made and enacted."[50]

By this time the assembly had divided into two houses. The council comprised the upper house and was dominated by friends and relatives of Lord Baltimore. The lower house, or assembly, represented the freemen, that is, the public. As the assembly gradually sought more power, friction between its members and the proprietor increased.

As a result, in 1670 Baltimore attempted to thwart the mostly Protestant opposition by signing a law that took voting rights away from those who owned less than fifty acres of land. This prevented the poorer inhabitants from voting. Andrews comments on Baltimore's puzzling behavior:

> Lord Baltimore had put himself on record in 1667 as sympathetic with "the poorer sort of planters . . ." [but]

. . . one of the grievances of the assembly was "the great charges [taxes] incurr'd to the public". . . . Perhaps the proprietor wished "to save their purses," by cutting down expenses, but the same result might have been achieved by reducing the number of deputies without disfranchising the poorer classes.[51]

Cecilius Calvert, the long-standing proprietor and second Lord Baltimore, died five years after signing this law. His son Charles, who was already the governor, became the third Lord Baltimore and the first to reside in the colony. Continuing his late father's efforts to gain more influence over the assembly, he limited the

Although he never left England, Cecilius Calvert was largely responsible for the early settlement and administration of Maryland.

number of representatives from each county. This further increased tension among the Maryland colonists. Then news came that Charles II had died. James II, his Catholic half brother, would assume the throne.

Reports of the Catholic king dissolving and disregarding acts of Parliament in England caused Protestants in Maryland to fear that the colony "was to be given over to Roman Catholicism."[52] It did not help matters that all of the important offices in the colony—governors, judges, military officials, tax collectors, and sheriffs—were largely held by Baltimore's family or by Protestants loyal to the proprietor.

REVOLUTION IN MARYLAND

In 1689 reports of the Glorious Revolution in England reached Maryland. James II

LIFE IN MARYLAND

In his book Maryland as a Proprietary Province, *Newton D. Mereness describes Maryland's lack of a unified community during the seventeenth century.*

"During the seventeenth century nearly all the people were . . . engaged in the cultivation of tobacco. Both large and small planters lived on their own plantations with a number of servants . . . proportionate to the size of the estate. Outside of the small settlement of houses—only thirty in number as late as the year 1678—that were scattered for five miles along the shore . . . town life was unknown. There were few mills and no factories. The trade was restricted to that which each planter carried on with the merchants of the mother country. There was an abundance of horses before the close of the [seventeenth] century, and yet the lack of good roads was a hindrance to travel. More than ninety per cent of the people were Protestants. . . . The depressing tendency [economic instability] of the tobacco culture and the remoteness of habitations from one another, together with the religious differences, resulted in the failure to found any public schools wherein a common interest might have been centered or wherein the social tie might have been knit among the children. Unlike what was the case in so many of the other colonies, the danger from the Indians was in Maryland insufficient to force the people together for protection."

The ascension of William and Mary put an end to Maryland's Catholic governed colony.

had been replaced by his daughter Mary, a Protestant, and William III, termed "the champion of Protestantism."[53] Lord Baltimore, who was in England at the time, immediately recognized William and Mary as the new rulers and sent instructions to his council in Maryland to do the same. Unfortunately, the message never arrived. When the council failed to proclaim William and Mary as the new monarchs, charges were made that the council had publicly denied their right to the throne.

Lord Baltimore's enemies were quick to take advantage of Protestant fears that James, the deposed king, would try to es-

tablish a Catholic foothold in Maryland. Protestants took up arms and seized control of the government. They sent two petitions to England. One requested that Lord Baltimore's proprietorship rights be abolished, and the other asked that Maryland be made a royal colony.

MARYLAND BECOMES ROYAL COLONY

Maryland officially became a royal colony on June 27, 1691. Lord Baltimore lost political control, but he retained the right to his land. Within eleven years the Church of England became the official church in Maryland, and Catholic priests were forbidden to hold masses until 1704.

In 1716 Benedict Leonard Calvert—the fourth Lord Baltimore—converted to Protestantism, and full governmental rights were restored to him. Maryland never again became a truly proprietary government, however, and for all intents and purposes, remained a royal colony until the American Revolution.

Although the first Lord Baltimore's dream of a colony in which Catholics and Protestants would live together in peace failed, his noble efforts struck the first blow for religious toleration in America and assured Maryland a unique place in the history of colonization.

Chapter

6 A King's Reward: The Carolinas

During England's civil war, British colonization of North America came to a near standstill. But in 1660, when Charles II was restored to the throne, colonization reached new heights. More than half of the thirteen colonies came into existence during Charles's reign—five within the first ten years. All of the post-Restoration colonies were founded as proprietorship (privately owned) colonies. Carolina was the first of these.

BEGINNINGS

Carolina had been the site of England's first colony in North America—the ill-fated Roanoke. After that failure, no further attempt was made to colonize the vast area that would become North and South Carolina until Charles II began his reign. Charles awarded Carolina to eight loyal friends as a reward for their help in rescuing him from exile.

These eight proprietors, all high-ranking nobles, had only one goal: to make money. They concentrated on northern Carolina because a small number of Virginians had already settled in the northernmost region of Carolina around Albemarle Sound. The proprietors planned to attract additional settlers from Virginia and the New England colonies rather than spend money to transport people from England.

THE GRAND MODEL

To encourage immigration, the proprietors drafted a plan of government that offered generous land grants and guaranteed freedom of worship and a legislative assembly. By 1669, however, the proprietors decided they had given the people too much power. They adopted an entirely new form of government called the Fundamental Constitutions, often referred to as the "Grand Model." This Grand Model was created by the philosopher John Locke, whose idea of a perfect society was one that would balance aristocracy and democracy.

The proprietors planned to create a nobility class by granting elaborate titles and large tracts of land. The common people below the nobility would be allowed to own land and slaves, but the proprietors and variously titled nobility would control the government. Understandably, this impractical form of government was never fully implemented. One crucial tenet of the Grand Model, however, would endure and haunt Carolina far into the future: "Every freeman of Carolina shall have absolute power and authority over his negro Slaves."[54]

NORTH CAROLINA—A DIFFERENT KIND OF COLONY

In their epilogue to Colonial North Carolina: A History, *authors Hugh T. Lefler and William S. Powell discuss the uniqueness of the North Carolina Colony.*

"The colony of North Carolina was an enigma to the . . . Proprietors as well as to the Crown and to many of the governors they appointed. None fully understood the . . . factors that divided the colony. . . . The divisive influences of geography, religion, and social status shaped the history of the whole colony. . . . Although there were families of local influence, there were none such as the Lees of Virginia. . . . The colony had no notable centers of commerce and culture such as existed in other colonies between Boston and Charleston. . . .

People in this isolated colony, with its disparate communities, became insular. . . . Little concern was shown for events transpiring elsewhere on the continent. Local government, with no interference from a higher authority, was the goal of most county leaders. . . .

As in other colonies, particularly those in the South, an overwhelming majority of the people made their living from farming and related industries. [North Carolina] was predominantly one of small towns and small landholders. . . . A few North Carolina planters owned more than a hundred slaves each, but the colony never developed a plantation aristocracy such as that in Virginia and South Carolina. Nor did North Carolina ever have as many indentured servants . . . as did her two neighbors. . . .

Unhappy experiences under governors sent from England, New York, or even South Carolina . . . convinced many . . . they could do better for themselves without outside aid. . . . [It would be] more than half a century after the Revolution [before] North Carolina finally began to break out of the cocoon in which she had wrapped herself during her colonial experience."

Albemarle never became the thriving settlement the proprietors envisioned. It was too isolated; wide swamps separated it from Virginia, and because its harbors were too shallow to accommodate large ships, trade with England was limited. The formation of pro- and antiproprietary groups led to unrest, and the proprietors began to look southward.

SOUTH CAROLINA

In 1669 the proprietors turned their full attention to southern Carolina because they believed it offered more potential for profit. They also decided on a new approach: Each proprietor contributed five hundred pounds to recruit men and women from England to settle in South Carolina. Three shiploads of colonists sailed from England in August 1669. When they reached South Carolina, they began laying out the town that would become Charlestown (Charleston).

Although the Charleston settlers did not suffer starving times, the first ten years were difficult. Food was in short supply because the initial settlers were not farmers. Also, they feared attack by the Spanish, who had an outpost at nearby St. Augustine. Soon, however, the large Westo Indian nation—which was interested in establishing trade relations with the Charleston settlers—joined them in an alliance against Spain. This substantially reduced fear of the Spanish.

THE GOOSE CREEK MEN

During Charleston's first decade, a sizable number of English settlers migrated from Barbados, an English-ruled colony in the West Indies. This group—called the Goose Creek men because they settled near Goose Creek—opposed proprietary government and sought to control local government themselves. They soon made up half the population of South Carolina.

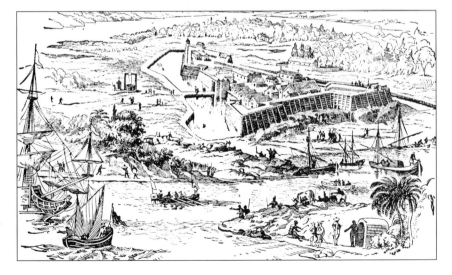

Settlers arrive in Charleston, the first settlement in South Carolina, founded in 1670.

The capture of Indians as slaves caused conflict between the Goose Creek men and the proprietors of the Carolinas.

The Goose Creek men demanded and were granted a representative assembly. From the outset, the assembly constantly disagreed with the council and the governor (both appointed by the proprietors). Conflict centered on three issues: the colonists' refusal to pay rental fees for use of the land, the Indian slave trade, and land distribution policies.

The proprietors were particularly upset over the ongoing Indian slave trade. In 1672 they had instituted laws against enslaving Indians "upon any occasion or pretense whatsoever."[55] But South Carolina traders had ignored these laws. The result was a series of Indian wars in which powerful Indian nations like the Westoes were eliminated, their people either killed or enslaved.

PROPRIETORS FIGHT BACK

By 1680 the Charleston settlers had improved their agricultural techniques and had begun selling furs and naval supplies (turpentine, tar, and ship spars) to England. Despite these signs of progress, the proprietors were discouraged. They had invested ten thousand pounds in the Carolina venture and had as yet received neither profit nor respect. Reluctant to concede failure, they resolved to recruit new settlers from the outside and institute reforms from within.

MINORITIES ARE WELCOMED

Before 1680 the majority of South Carolina's settlers were English, either emigrating from the West Indies or from England itself. The proprietors now concentrated on recruiting religious dissidents who were eager to leave their respective countries to escape persecution. Between 1682 and 1685, some five hundred English Presbyterians and Baptists arrived in South Carolina. And when emigration from Britain decreased, Huguenots (French Protestants) fleeing religious persecution in France took up the slack.

With this new mix of people, the proprietors instigated reform policies. They tried to end Indian slave trade, attempted to make land distribution more equitable, and sought to stop Carolinians from trading with pirates. (The Carolinas had the worst reputation for piracy of all the continental colonies.) Unfortunately, the reform attempts only widened the gap between pro- and antiproprietary factions. The proprietary party was made up mostly of English dissenters—the newcomers to the colony. They supported the proprietors because they were grateful for the religious toleration that had given them refuge. And of course as newcomers, they were not yet involved in Indian slave trade or trade with pirates, so they had nothing to lose economically.

The antiproprietary party consisted mainly of Goose Creek men—the old-timers who held most of the political positions and controlled the government. They saw no wrong in trading with pirates, and they had little tolerance for those who did not belong to the Church of England. After three years of attempted reforms amidst these warring factions, the proprietors had made little progress.

Indian Uprisings in the Carolinas

Carolina colonists consistently cheated and swindled Native Americans in trade agreements until finally the Indians were driven to revolt. Historian M. Eugene Sirmans describes the wars that followed in his book Colonial South Carolina.

"The Yamasee War, the longest and perhaps the costliest Indian war in Carolina history, involved nearly every Indian nation that traded with South Carolina—Creeks, Choctaws, and Catawbas as well as Yamasees. . . . Unlike most colonial Indian wars, the expansion of white settlement was not a primary cause of the Yamasee War. . . . The sole cause . . . was South Carolina's failure to regulate the Indian trade, and the Indians were driven to revolt by their resentment of the abuses practiced by the traders. . . .

The war began on . . . April 15, 1715, when the Yamasees fell upon the frontier settlements near Port Royal with sickening suddenness and murdered about a hundred whites. . . . The attack on Port Royal was the signal for a massive uprising among the southern Indians. . . . Frightened settlers from all over South Carolina . . . fled to Charles Town. For half a year the town resembled a fortress. . . . The signing of [a] Cherokee treaty turned the tide of the Yamasee War in South Carolina's favor. . . . However . . . the Creeks, Yamasees and Choctaws . . . continued to attack frontier settlements throughout 1716."

Indentured Servants and Apprentices in North Carolina

This description of indentures and apprenticeships in North Carolina is excerpted from editor Hugh Talmage Lefler's North Carolina History Told by Contemporaries.

"It has been estimated that there were more indentured white servants than black slaves in the first half century of [North Carolina's] existence. Many . . . were 'redemptioners,'. . . people who had voluntarily 'bound' themselves to some master for a fixed number of years in order to 'redeem' their passage to this country. Some were political prisoners; some were convicts sold into bondage in lieu of jail service; while others were persons who had been kidnapped in English cities and sent to America. The period of service depended on the contract, usually being three to five years. . . . Many of the indentures provided that the servant should be taught a trade and to read and write. . . .

There is a striking similarity between the apprenticeship system of the eighteenth and nineteenth centuries and the indentures of the seventeenth century. . . . Children were apprenticed, with the consent of their parents; orphans and illegitimate children were frequently 'bound out' by order of the court; while Negro children were often apprenticed to learn 'plantation business.'

Most of the indentures provided that the master should teach the apprentice to read and write. This provision was stricken out of some of the contracts which involved Negro children."

Rice and Slavery

The proprietors and the settlers had persistently searched for a staple product that would ensure South Carolina's prosperity, much like tobacco had done for Virginia and Maryland. They found it in rice. A pamphlet published in 1666 states that "the Meadows [in South Carolina] are very proper for Rice,"[56] but it took another quarter century before the colonists learned how to successfully cultivate the plant.

The prosperity that rice brought to South Carolina settlers changed their lives in several ways. First of all, it put an end to the pirate trade. Pirates were no longer tolerated because now the settlers' own rice shipments had become targets. Secondly, as Charleston grew in size and wealth, a class society developed because not everyone profited. Small farmers in outlying areas, for instance, remained poor. Wealth became the measure of status. Thirdly, because the cultivation of rice required a huge labor force, there was a marked increase in the number of African slaves. Historian M. Eugene Sirmans discusses this in *Colonial South Carolina:*

> The most impressive evidence of a South Carolinian's prosperity was the number of Negro slaves he owned. Sir Nathaniel Johnson became the first of the great slaveowners when he brought more than a hundred Negroes into the colony in the early 1690s. . . . Other planters emulated Johnson's example. . . . The Negro population grew so fast that as early as 1699 . . . there were four Negroes in South Carolina for every white.[57]

FORGOTTEN NORTH CAROLINA

Meanwhile, conditions in North Carolina had gone from bad to worse. The proprietors paid little attention to the struggling colony, and calamities in the form of hurricanes, drought, and illness dealt one blow after another. As one official noted, "It hath pleased God . . . to inflict such a generall calamitie upon the inhabitants . . . that for severall years they [have] nott injoyed the fruitts of their labours which causes them generally to growne under the [burden] of poverty and many times famine."[58]

North Carolina was dependent on Virginia ports for exporting tobacco, its only cash crop. But Virginia charged such exorbitant fees that the settlers turned to smuggling to survive economically. Massachusetts and Rhode Island traders could maneuver small shallow-water vessels

Rice cultivation ensured South Carolina's prosperity and changed the settlers' lives in several ways.

A Letter from "Charles Town"

Thomas Newe, a graduate of Oxford University, came to Carolina in 1682 to make his fortune. His account of the war between the traders and the Westo Indians favors the traders. Newe died a year after writing this letter to his father, which is quoted in editor David Hawke's U.S. Colonial History: Readings and Documents.

"Most Honored Father: By the providence of God, after a long and tedious passage, we came to . . . Charles Town at ten in the night. . . . [During the voyage] I had my health very well . . . , but most of the other passengers were much troubled with the scurvy. Of sixty-two that came out of England we lost three. Two of them were seamen; one died of scurvy, the other fell overboard. The third was a woman in childbed [childbirth]; her child died shortly after her. . . .

The land near the seaside is generally a light and sandy ground, but up in the country they say there is very good land, and the farther up the better. But that which . . . doth . . . hinder the settling farther up is a war that they are engaged in against a tribe of barbarous Indians, being not above sixty in number, but by reason of their great growth and cruelty in feeding on their neighbors they are terrible to all other Indians, of which there are about forty . . . kingdoms. . . . We are at peace with all but those common enemies of mankind, those man-eaters before mentioned, by name the Westos. . . .

If they can make good wine here, which they have great hopes of . . . the place will flourish exceedingly; but if the vines do not prosper, I question whether it will ever be any great place of trade."

through North Carolina inlets. They would pick up tobacco, take it to New England, and then reship it directly to Ireland, Holland, France, Spain, and Scotland. In this way, English export duties, required under the Navigation Acts, were avoided.

In 1673 England tried to stop these violations by passing a law that required ships traveling from one colonial port to another to pay a customs duty. Local customs collectors were appointed, but they showed little enthusiasm for performing their duties. They knew that if the law was enforced, New England merchants would not send ships to North Carolina.

Culpepper's Rebellion

Finally, England sent Thomas Miller—a newly assigned deputy governor—to see that the customs fees were collected. The North Carolinians did not welcome him. Hostility increased when Miller called for the election of a new assembly and tried to prevent those who opposed him from voting. Miller used his position to harass his enemies, but he went too far when he arrested George Durant, one of North Carolina's oldest preproprietary settlers. People came from all over the colony to help Durant. The leaders, among them colonist John Culpepper, ousted Miller and set up a revolutionary government. They conducted the colony's business in an orderly manner, but "after their own fashion."[59] Culpepper's Rebellion, as it came to be called, was one of the earliest uprisings of American colonists against a government they considered unjust.

POLES APART

Marked differences between the two provinces of Carolina had always existed, and by the beginning of the eighteenth century the gap had widened. North Carolina was populated largely by former indentured servants and other poor whites who had been squeezed out of Virginia by the low price of tobacco. North Carolina's small landowners were rugged, radical individualists dedicated to the principles of personal liberty. South Carolina, with its abundance of landowners and commercial success, was a conservative, aristocratic society. Charleston was a sophisticated and cosmopolitan city while North Carolina had no town at all.

THE CAROLINAS GO ROYAL

Despite their dissimilarity, colonists in North and South Carolina had one thing in common: They both resented the proprietors. It angered them that the proprietors had offered little help against massive Native American uprisings that had begun in 1715 with the Tuscarora Indians in North Carolina and continued with the Yamassee

King George I responded to colonists' demands and made North and South Carolina royal colonies.

War in 1717. Thus in 1719, fearing that the proprietors had abandoned the colony to its enemies—the Spanish in Florida, the French in Louisiana, and the Native Americans—South Carolinians asked England to make South Carolina a royal colony.

In 1729 the monarchy paid the proprietors a large sum of money for their land, and King George I declared both North and South Carolina royal colonies. After some initial problems, South Carolina continued to prosper. In North Carolina, growth and economic success came more slowly, but in 1776 it would be the first colony to instruct its delegates to vote for independence from England.

Chapter 7

A Mixed Bag: New York and New Jersey

By 1664 England had a chain of colonies along the Atlantic Coast interrupted only by New Netherland, a colony founded by Holland forty years earlier. England and Holland were already at war in Europe, and the Dutch presence in North America disturbed England. Charles II, the reigning monarch, was advised that New Netherland was interfering with British trade and that its people were discontented under the rule of their governor, Peter Stuyvesant. As a result, Charles granted New Netherland to his brother James, the duke of York, as a proprietary estate. All James had to do was conquer it.

NEW NETHERLAND BECOMES NEW YORK

James had no difficulty collecting his prize. He sent a fleet of ships commanded by Richard Nicolls, his appointed deputy governor, to seize the colony. Nicolls arrived in the New Amsterdam harbor on August 18, 1664, and ordered the Dutch to

With their surrender in 1664, the Dutch colony of New Netherland became the English colony of New York.

surrender. Stuyvesant pleaded with his people to resist, but they refused. New Netherland went from Dutch rule to English without a shot being fired. By October the colony had been renamed New York.

James, the duke of York, was now sole proprietor of all the land between the Connecticut and Delaware Rivers, including Long Island and part of Maine. His unusual charter—the only one ever issued to a possible heir to the throne—contained no provision for a representative assembly such as had been required by other colonial charters, and the duke refused to allow one.

In other respects, James's government was a liberal one. Land titles were recog-

---

DUTCH HERITAGE IN NEW YORK

Although the English took over the land occupied by Holland, forty years of Dutch culture left its imprint. Historian David Hawke describes America's Dutch legacy in his book The Colonial Experience.

"The Dutch . . . left their strongest impress on social customs. Sleighing, coasting, and ice skating count among their innovations. . . . They gave the Easter egg and Santa Claus to America. St. Nicholas was the patron saint of New Amsterdam, and the children set out their shoes on his birthday, December 6, to receive his gifts; gradually the custom shifted to Christmas Eve. . . .

The Dutch gave to the city of New York its colors and seal and to the state some of its most distinguished names: the Van Rensselaers, Van Burens, and Roosevelts. And they gave to the nation several words from their language: 'bowery' (farm), 'brief' (letter), 'spook' (ghost). . . . 'Cruller' and 'cooky' are Dutch words, as are 'boss,' [and] 'dope' (as in 'give me the inside dope')."

Ice skating is one of the many examples of Dutch influence in America.

nized and complete religious freedom was guaranteed. He ordered Governor Nicolls to treat the conquered Dutch with "humanity and gentleness"[60] and gave them the choice of remaining in New York or returning to Holland. Almost all, including Peter Stuyvesant, elected to remain.

DEMAND FOR COLONIAL ASSEMBLY

Richard Nicolls, an able governor, had great success with the Dutch inhabitants. But the Puritan emigrants from New England, "overwhelmingly English by race and closely attached to New England by sympathies,"[61] presented a greater challenge. They complained that they were "inslav'd under an Arbitrary power,"[62] and they demanded local self-government—a request Nicolls could not grant because the duke refused to allow a representative assembly.

Over the next eight years, the Puritans continued to protest the lack of representation. Some refused to pay taxes because they had been levied without their consent. In 1674 Sir Edmund Andros was appointed governor. He ultimately suggested to the duke of York that taxes might be easier to collect if he would permit a representative assembly, and the duke indicated he might consider it. In 1676 he wrote to Andros,

> I . . . suspect [assemblies] would be of dangerous consequence, nothing being more knowne than the aptness [tendency] of such bodyes to

assume to themselves many priviledges which prove destructive to . . . the peace of the government. . . . But . . . if you continue of the same opinion, I shall . . . consider . . . any proposalls you shall send to that purpose.[63]

Seven years later, however, New York still had no popular assembly.

A DUKE BECOMES A KING

In 1683 James, duke of York, recalled Andros and appointed Thomas Dongan governor. Dongan was a personal friend and an Irish Catholic. (James, by this time, had converted to Catholicism.) To counteract the inevitable protests that would arise from appointing a Catholic, James instructed Dongan to call a general assembly

> of all the freeholders [landowners] by the persons who they shall choose to represent them . . . to [consult] with yourself and the . . . Council what laws are fit and necessary to be made . . . for the good . . . government of the . . . Colony and . . . of all the inhabitants thereof.[64]

On September 13, 1683, for the first time in the history of New York, a legislative assembly convened. The assembly would be short-lived, however; on February 6, 1685, Charles II died and James, duke of York, became James II, king of England.

With James being both the proprietor and now the king, New York changed from a proprietary colony to a royal colony, making it subject to the king and other executive branches of government in England. As king, James abolished the newly formed assembly. Soon afterward, he created the Dominion of New England.

Three years after James assumed the throne, tensions in New York were nearing the boiling point. The people had countless complaints: no representative assembly, taxes levied without consent, monopolies that placed profits in the hands of a few, and resentment against the Navigation Acts legislated by England to control trade. Not surprisingly, when news reached New York that James had been forced from the throne, the colony staged its own revolution.

LEISLER'S REBELLION

On May 31, 1689, the New York City militia seized control of the fort that housed the colony's government offices. Delegates were summoned from seven counties to consider ways to maintain the revolutionary government. These delegates did not represent all parts of New York. Nonetheless, they named German immigrant and militia captain Jacob Leisler commander in chief of the colony. He was given power to act in legal, military, and administrative matters. Because Leisler enjoyed widespread support, "the thirteen months of Leislerian government . . . was not a time of mob rule. Leisler and his associates . . . allowed neither lawlessness nor anarchy to prevail."[65]

Leisler's reign ended tragically in 1691, however, when new monarchs William

Despite maintaining order during a turbulent time, Jacob Leisler was sentenced as a traitor.

and Mary sent a royal governor and soldiers to New York to reestablish royal authority. When the governor's military commander asked Leisler to surrender the militia, he refused to surrender to anyone but the governor himself.

Leisler's enemies—New York's wealthy merchants and landowners who had incurred financial losses under the revolutionary government—used this incident to convince the Crown that Leisler was a rebel. He was tried for treason, found guilty, and hanged on May 16, 1691. (Parliament reversed the conviction four years later.) "The act of execution was not only merciless," historian Charles M. Andrews writes, "but it was a blunder, for it kept alive the prevailing animosities for years to come."[66]

New York's first royal governor arrived with the authority to "call generall Assemblies of the Inhabitants being Freeholders

LEISLER: REBEL OR SAINT?

Jacob Leisler's motives for his takeover of the New York government have been both defended and condemned by historians. Charles M. Andrews presents a portrait of Leisler in The Colonial Period of American History.

"Leisler has always been a troublesome character to interpret because of the difficulties met in estimating his motives and accomplishments. . . . There is no good reason in his case for either defense or attack. Leisler . . . was in the same class . . . [as other] men who came to the front in a time of conflict. . . . The combination of . . . circumstances [in New York] furnished an opportunity for someone to assume the leadership—someone possessed of boldness, confidence in the justness of his cause, acting in accord with the spirit of the English revolution, and holding certain definite notions regarding the rights of Englishmen. . . .

Such a man was Leisler. He had courage, capacity for work, a forceful personality, and . . . organizing ability. He found followers, not only among the working classes—the bricklayers, blockmakers, farmers, traders, officers of the militia, and roving agitators of the time, but also among the merchants, traders, and professional classes, notably the Dutch. In carrying out his ambitions he was domineering, revengeful, and often demagogic, proclaiming martial law, inflicting heavy penalties, and employing terrorizing methods. In defense of his usurpation he . . . built up his claim to govern on what he believed, or pretended to believe was a royal mandate to him. . . . Inevitably, as with leaders in all revolutions . . . a zest for power became an increasingly dominant motive. As this tendency became manifest [apparent], his following, grown fearful, fell off; the towns in Queens County, Long Island, repudiated his claims and charged him with tyranny . . . and within Manhattan itself merchants and traders began to send urgent petitions to England against him."

within your Government, according to the usage [custom] of our other Plantations in America."[67] On March 30, 1691, such an assembly was called. Whether the long-sought representative assembly was a result of what came to be known as Leisler's Rebellion remains a question. But whatever the answer, New York—complete with a royal governor, a council, and a popular assembly—was prepared to embark on a new era in its history.

NEW JERSEY

New Jersey's history is the most complicated of the thirteen colonies. Like New York, it began as part of New Netherland. After conquering New Netherland, James, duke of York, gave a large section to his friends Sir George Carteret and Lord John Berkeley (two of the eight Carolina proprietors). Carteret, who had been born on England's Isle of Jersey, named the area New Jersey.

Berkeley and Carteret promised immigrants to New Jersey freedom of religion, a representative assembly, and the power to levy taxes. Immigrants were not, however, allowed to purchase land outright. They were granted land for their use, but they had to pay an annual rental fee to the proprietors. These fees were waived until 1670, but this system of land distribution would generate problems.

NEW JERSEY SETTLERS

Neither Berkeley nor Carteret came to New Jersey. Instead, they sent Philip Car-

teret, a cousin of Sir George, to govern for them. When Governor Carteret and thirty immigrants arrived at Elizabethtown, New Jersey, in July 1665, only four families occupied the town. Puritans from Long Island had recently established three other towns—Middletown, Shrewsbury, and Woodbridge—but the overall population was scant and confined to eastern New Jersey. The western part remained unsettled.

The Puritan towns were a result of land granted under the so-called Monmouth Patent by New York governor Richard Nicolls. Nicolls made the grants before he

Sir George Carteret was one of the two original proprietors of New Jersey.

The Glorious Revolution and Leisler's Rebellion

The Glorious Revolution in England, which toppled James II from the throne, led to Leisler's Rebellion, an uprising of the people of New York. The following account of a council meeting held May 31, 1689, the day of the rebellion, is quoted in The Glorious Revolution in America, *edited by Michael G. Hall, Lawrence H. Leder, and Michael G. Kammen.*

"The Inhabitants of New Yorke ryseing [rising] this afternoone have taken possession of the Fortt, disarmed the souldiers, and came with a squadron armed in Courtt demanding the keys of the Garrison and with force would and will have them. . . . The Lieutenant Governor seeing himself forced asked the advice of this Board [Council] what to doe in this confused businesse.

This Board . . . to hinder and prevent bloodshed and further mischiefe and . . . endeavouring to quiett the minds of the people think it best considering they being forced to itt to let them have the keys.

[In answer to] His Honor [the lieutenant governor] proposeing to this Board what way or whether any meanes may be found to reduce this people from their riseing or what other method may bee taken to bring them to their former obedience, This Board are of opinion that there is noe way to reduce them by force but their [the Board's] advice is since they are rise on their owne heads [by their own efforts] without any aid that they be lett alone for some time."

learned that New Jersey had been given away by the duke of York. These double grants led to ongoing disputes over land-ownership, some of which would not be resolved until well into the eighteenth century.

Additional problems developed in 1670 when the seven-year deferment of land rental fees ended and the proprietors tried to collect the rents. The Puritan immigrants to New Jersey were accustomed to self-government. They simply could not conceive of a proprietary government that wanted to charge them rent on their own land. "How could Governor Carteret say that . . . the Monmouth Patent was of no account and that the lands they . . . held by deed . . . were not theirs but belonged to the proprietors?"[68] Finally, the duke of York intervened and officially declared titles to any land granted under the Monmouth Patent to be illegal. However, this did not end the confusion surrounding New Jersey's government because the colony would soon undergo a significant change.

THE DIVISION OF NEW JERSEY

In 1674 Lord Berkeley, who needed money to pay debts, sold his half of New Jersey to a group of Quakers, one of whom was William Penn, the future founder of Pennsylvania. Sir George Carteret, the remaining original proprietor, and the new Quaker proprietors agreed to divide New Jersey into two parts. Carteret became the sole owner of East New Jersey, and the Quakers took unsettled West New Jersey.

The Quakers immediately made plans to settle West New Jersey. This was easily accomplished because Quakers, suffering harsh persecution in England, were eager to immigrate to the New World. Population in West New Jersey increased rapidly.

ACCOUNT OF EAST NEW JERSEY

In 1684 three settlers wrote an account of the East New Jersey Colony; however, their description is somewhat biased because its intent was to attract settlers. These excerpts are from American History Told by Contemporaries, *edited by Albert Bushnell Hart.*

"For the encouragement of all our countrymen who may be inclinable to come into this Countrey [we give] you this brief and true account of it. . . . A great deal of [the land] is naturally clear of wood, And what is not so, is easily cleared, the trees being but small and a good distance from one another, so that the Land yet untaken up [unsettled] . . . is easier to clear than that which is taken up, the Towns that are already seated [established], being seated in the woodiest places.

The Merchants in *New York*, both *Dutch* and *English*, have many of them taken up land among us, and settled Plantations in this Countrey, and severall from that Collony are desiring to come and take up land among us, though they might have land in their own Collony without paying Quitt rents [land rental fees]. . . .

There be People of several sorts of Religion, but few very Zealous. The People being mostly *New England* men, doe mostly incline to their way, and in every Town there is a meeting house where they worship publickly every Week. . . .

There are few *Indian Natives* in this Countrey. There strength is inconsiderably, they live in the Woods, and have small towns in some places far up in the Countrey. . . . They have *Kings* among themselves to govern them. For *Religion*, they have none at all."

Quakers settle the area of western New Jersey.

In 1677 the Quaker proprietors issued the "Laws, Concessions, and Agreements," a document that "put the *power* [of government] *in the people.*"[69] With this new government, West New Jersey appeared to have achieved stability as a separate province. This could not be said of East New Jersey.

Sir George Carteret, the proprietor of East New Jersey, died in 1680. He left his proprietorship to his wife and his trustees with instructions to sell the land to pay his debts. East New Jersey was sold at public auction in 1682 to twelve men, most of whom were Quakers. To lighten expenses, the twelve men sold off land to others. Ultimately, twenty-four proprietors of varied political, social, and religious views owned and governed East New Jersey, by then inhabited by over five thousand people.

Some of the East New Jersey proprietors were irresponsible in disposing of their property. Land was sold or given away without boundaries being properly surveyed. Speculators often appropriated the best land with their main objective being to sell it for a profit rather than improve it. "Land troubles lay at the very heart of the East New Jersey situation," historian Charles M. Andrews writes, "for they concerned not only the title to the soil but the right of the people at large to have a part in government."[70]

REVOLUTION AGAINST THE PROPRIETARY GOVERNMENT

The proprietary government was increasingly resented in both Jerseys. Even in relatively peaceful West New Jersey, inhabitants challenged the right of proprietors to govern.

In 1685, when the duke of York became king and created the Dominion of New England, the proprietors of both East and West New Jersey were forced to surrender all governing authority. The Glorious Revolution ended the dominion in 1688, however, and the proprietors—who had retained their land rights—resumed control of the Jersey governments.

Resentment toward the proprietors had not lessened during the interval of nonproprietary government. If anything, it had escalated. Consequently, when the proprietors resumed control, rioting occurred in both East and West New Jersey. The situation quickly approached anarchy. Unable to maintain political order, the proprietors relinquished their governing powers; on April 17, 1702, East and West New Jersey were united as the royal province of New Jersey.

Chapter

8 The Holy Experiment: Pennsylvania and Delaware

Pennsylvania was the last colony founded in the seventeenth century. Its story, for the most part, is the story of William Penn, its idealistic founder. Penn was born in 1644 into an aristocratic and wealthy English family. His family belonged to the Church of England, but Penn abandoned the Anglican church at age sixteen, when he discovered the Quaker faith that would change his life.

THE QUAKERS

Quakerism had begun in the mid–seventeenth century under the formal name Society of Friends. Members referred to each other as "Friends," but outsiders, who ridiculed them for admonishing people "to quake in the presence of the Lord," called them "Quakers." The Quakers were considered a threat in England because they opposed the Church of England and refused to pay taxes for its support. As pacifists, they also refused to serve in the military. Consequently, thousands of Quakers were jailed or fined heavily for practicing their faith. Penn himself was jailed a number of times.

By 1671 England's harried Quakers began looking to the New World for refuge. Some went to Rhode Island, where they were accepted; others went to Massachusetts, where they were persecuted in the

Persecuted for their beliefs in England, the Quakers settled in Pennsylvania and in other colonies that allowed religious freedom.

same manner as in England. In 1674, when Quakers purchased West New Jersey, many English Quakers migrated there.

COLLECTING A DEBT

William Penn, who was actively involved in the colonization of New Jersey, dreamed of establishing a colony large enough to be a sanctuary for all people suffering persecution. Penn's father had once loaned King Charles II a large sum of money that was never repaid. In 1681, Penn petitioned the king for a grant of land in America as payment of the "debts due to him and his father from the Crown."[71]

On March 4, 1681, the king signed the charter of Pennsylvania, granting William Penn an area of land as large as England itself. About two thousand Dutch and Swedish settlers already lived in Pennsylvania, most of them on the west shore of Delaware Bay—the area that would become Delaware. The king issued a declaration to these inhabitants that they must obey Penn as the absolute proprietor and governor.

Penn did not go to America immediately, but he sent his cousin William Markham, as his deputy governor. He instructed Markham to read the king's proclamation to the Delaware Bay inhabitants along with a letter written by Penn. The letter read in part,

> I wish . . . to let you know that it hath pleased God . . . to cast you within my lot and care. . . . I hope you will not be troubled at your change, and the King's choice, for . . . you shall be governed by *laws of your own making, and live [as] a free,* and if you will, *a sober and industrious* people. I shall not usurp the right of any, or oppress his person.[72]

Later that year Penn dispatched four commissioners and a small number of settlers to Pennsylvania to choose a suitable site for a town. Recognizing that the Native Americans were the true owners of the land, Penn cautioned the commissioners to "be tender [careful] of offending the Indians."[73] He also gave them a letter to read to the chiefs of the resident Lenape tribe. In the letter, Penn wrote: "I am very sensible [aware] of the unkindness and injustice which have been too much exercised toward you by the people of these parts of the world."[74]

THE FRAME OF GOVERNMENT

In the meantime, Penn worked on drafting what he called the Frame of Government for his colony. He believed in individual liberty and in the right of citizens to voice dissent. "Governments . . . depend upon men [rather] than men upon governments," he wrote. "Let men be good, and the government cannot be bad."[75]

The Frame of Government was completed in April 1682. It provided for a provincial council and an assembly. The council would propose all laws; the assembly could approve or reject the laws, but it could not initiate them. Both bodies would be elected by the freemen (male landowners) in the colony.

PENN'S LETTER TO THE NATIVE AMERICANS

William Penn's humane treatment of the Indians was unmatched by any other colonial leader. Before Penn even left England, he sent a letter with his representatives to be read to the Native Americans. The letter is reprinted in Samuel M. Janney's The Life of William Penn.

"My Friends: There is one great God . . . that hath made the world and all things therein, to whom you, and I, and all people owe their being . . . and to whom you and I must one day give an account. . . .

Now this great God hath been pleased to make me concerned in your part of the world; and the king of the country where I live hath given me a great province therein; but I desire to enjoy it with your love and consent, that we may always live together as neighbours and friends. . . .

I am very sensible of the unkindness and injustice which have been too much exercised toward you by the people of these parts of the world, who have sought . . . to make advantages by you, rather than to be examples of justice and goodness. . . . This I hear hath been a matter of trouble to you, and caused great . . . animosities, sometimes to the shedding of blood. . . .

But I am not such a man, as is well known in my own country. I have great love and regard toward you, and desire to win and gain your love and friendship by a kind, just, and peaceable life; and the people I send are of the same mind, and shall in all things behave themselves accordingly, and if in any thing any shall offend you . . . you shall have a full and speedy satisfaction for the same. . . .

I shall shortly come to see you myself, at which time we may more largely and freely confer . . . [on] these matters. In the mean time I have sent my commissioners to treat [talk] with you about land and a firm league of peace. Let me desire you to be kind to them and to the people, and receive the presents . . . which I have sent you, as a testimony of my good will . . . , and of my resolution to live justly, peaceably, and friendly with you."

Penn was generous with land grants, and he opened the colony to everyone. There was no state church. Every person could worship according to individual conscience, although only Christians could hold office.

The seal of the colony of Pennsylvania.

TAKING CHARGE

On October 27, 1682, William Penn and approximately one hundred colonists (mostly "Friends") arrived in America. After stopping briefly in Delaware, they proceeded to Philadelphia where the commissioners had laid out the town according to Penn's instructions.

William Penn remained in Pennsylvania for only two years. During that time he enacted laws that protected not only the liberties of the English inhabitants but those of all nationalities. Pennsylvania's liberal government made it attractive to immigrants. By January 1684 four thousand persons were residing in the colony.

That year, however, Penn had to return to England to settle a boundary dispute between Pennsylvania and Maryland. Entrusting his executive powers to the Pennsylvania council, he departed on August 12.

"SORRY AT HEART"

Aboard the ship to England, Penn wrote to the colonists: "O, you are now come to a quiet land; provoke not the Lord to trouble it!"[76] Unfortunately, Penn's plea would go unheeded.

Friction had always existed between Pennsylvania's council and assembly, but it escalated after Penn's departure. The assembly constantly sought more power, and the council grew increasingly arrogant in its dealings with the assembly and with Penn himself. Penn wrote letters beseeching the officers of his government to work together in harmony, but the letters went unanswered. "I am sorry at heart that my letters to the council are so slightly regarded,"[77] Penn wrote to a friend.

By 1687 Penn, still in England, was driven to make a change in Pennsylvania's government. He took away the council's executive power and appointed five commissioners to take charge. Still, the political bickering continued. When Penn had trouble collecting the rental fees that were due to him for use of the land, he decided to put executive control into the hands of one man. Strangely, he selected Captain John Blackwell, a Puritan and a military man. "For your ease," Penn wrote the commissioners, "I have appointed one that is not a Friend, but a grave, sober, wise man. . . . Let him see

PENN'S FIRST FRAME OF GOVERNMENT

William Penn's original model of government proved unworkable, but many of its ideas were original for the time. Its preface explained Penn's thoughts on the principles of government. These excerpts are from The Annals of America, *edited by Mortimer J. Adler.*

"[As to] particular frames and models [of government] . . . I do not find a model in the world that time, place, and some singular [unusual] emergencies have not necessarily altered; nor is it easy to frame a civil government that shall serve all places alike. . . .

I know what is said by the . . . admirers of monarchy, aristocracy, and democracy, which are the . . . three common ideas of government. . . . But I choose to solve the controversy with this small distinction, and it belongs to all three: Any government is free to the people under it . . . where the laws rule, and the people are [a] party to those laws. . . .

Governments, like clocks, go from the motion men give them; and as governments are made and moved by men, so by them they are ruined too. . . . Governments rather depend upon men than men upon governments. Let men be good, and the government cannot be bad. . . .

To . . . secure [protect] the people from the abuse of power . . . [is what] I humbly pray and hope God will please to make the lot [fate] of . . . Pennsylvania."

Although not successful at the time, William Penn's ideas of government would later influence the leaders of the American Revolution.

what he can do a while. . . . If he do not please you, he shall be laid aside."[78]

But Blackwell could not get along with the Quakers, and in desperation Penn decided to allow the assembly and council to elect their own governor. This had a calming effect, and the two governing bodies settled down to a more acceptable legislative routine. That they expected Penn to return soon also helped stabilize the situation.

Penn Loses and Regains His Proprietorship

However, by this time James II—Penn's friend and protector for many years—had been forced from the throne in England. Penn could not return to Pennsylvania because he was suspected of plotting to restore James to the throne. Twice in 1690 he was arrested and put on trial for treason; each time he was released due to insufficient evidence.

To make matters worse, England had gone to war with France, and the upper regions of New York were threatened by French Canadians and their Indian allies. New York asked Pennsylvania to send men to help them, but the pacifist Quaker government refused. Angered by this, the Crown suspended Penn's charter and made Pennsylvania a royal colony.

Pennsylvania remained a royal colony for two years. During that time, Penn repeatedly petitioned for restoration of his proprietary rights. In August 1694 the monarchy agreed to restore his rights on the condition that he return to Pennsylvania, straighten out its government, and promise to aid in the defense of New York. Penn agreed to all of the conditions.

A member of the Quaker religion, William Penn wanted Pennsylvania to be a refuge for people of all faiths and nationalities.

Charter of Privileges

In 1699, after an absence of fifteen years, William Penn returned to Pennsylvania. The colony was prosperous, but the political situation remained in disarray. Penn told the assembly members: "If there be anything that jarrs, alter it; if you want a law for this or that, prepare itt."[79] Taking Penn at his word, the assembly and council began preparing a new plan of government.

Penn's main concession was agreeing to exclude the council from the legislative process. This put the government in the hands of the assembly and made the Pennsylvania government unicameral, or one house. Penn retained the right to appoint the governor.

A part of Pennsylvania for a number of years, Delaware was originally settled by colonists from Sweden.

On October 28, 1701, the Charter of Privileges (misnamed because it was not a charter but a new Frame of Government) was adopted. The document, which served as the colony's constitution until the American Revolution, virtually ended proprietary rule in Pennsylvania.

William Penn's "holy experiment" did not succeed as he had visualized it. However, Pennsylvania was one of the most successful of the thirteen colonies, and its government based on civil and religious liberty was a giant step toward enlightenment in government.

DELAWARE

The tiny section of Pennsylvania that became Delaware has a complex history. First claimed by the Dutch, then settled by Swedes, it came under English rule when the duke of York seized New Netherland in 1660. Twenty-two years later, the duke deeded the area later known as Delaware to William Penn.

When Penn arrived at New Castle—the colonial capital of Delaware—in 1682, he assured the people there that they would enjoy the same privileges as those living in Pennsylvania and would be governed only by laws consented to by themselves and their representatives.

THE ACT OF UNION

The Delaware inhabitants wanted Penn's promise made official. Consequently, when the first Pennsylvania General Assembly convened in March 1683, Delaware petitioned for an Act of Union

GERMAN SETTLERS IN PENNSYLVANIA

In 1683 German Mennonites founded Germantown, Pennsylvania. Francis D. Pastorius, an agent for the land company that sponsored the venture, wrote this account in 1700. It is excerpted from The Annals of America, *edited by Mortimer J. Adler.*

"The governor, William Penn, laid out the city of Philadelphia between the two rivers Delaware and Schuylkill, naming it with the pious wish . . . that its inhabitants might dwell together in brotherly love and unity. . . .

The inhabitants may be divided into three classes: (1) the aborigines, or, as they are called, the savages; (2) those Christians who have been in the country for years and are called old settlers; (3) the newly arrived colonists of the different companies. . . .

The aborigines of this country had their own chiefs and kings. We Christians acknowledge as our . . . chief magistrate the . . . Hon. William Penn, to whom this region was granted . . . by His Majesty of England, Charles II, with the express command that all the previous and future colonists should be subject to Penn's laws and jurisdiction.

This wise and truly pious . . . governor did not, however, take possession of the province thus granted without having first . . . duly purchased from, the natives . . . the various regions of Pennsylvania. . . . I therefore have purchased from him some 30,000 acres for my German colony.

William Penn is . . . of the sects of Friends, or Quakers . . . , but he has granted to everyone free . . . exercise of their opinions and . . . complete liberty of conscience. . . .

In my newly laid out Germantown there are already sixty-four families in a very prosperous condition. . . . We are employing the wild inhabitants . . . and we ourselves are gradually learning their language, so to instruct them in the religion of Christ."

"humbly desiring . . . incorporation with the province of Pennsylvania, in order to . . . [enjoy] . . . all the rights and privileges of that province."[80]

In December Penn signed into law a bill granting the incorporation. The law also decreed that Delaware would have equal representation with Pennsylvania in the assembly and the council. Thus, Delaware officially became part of Pennsylvania, but it would be an uneasy association.

A Union Doomed to Fail

Multiple religious and cultural differences existed among the peoples of Delaware and Pennsylvania. Inhabitants of Pennsylvania were almost all Quakers, while in Delaware the predominant religions were Lutheranism and Calvinism. The colonists in Pennsylvania were of English descent, but in Delaware the majority were Dutch and Swedish. Also, the commercial success of Pennsylvania, particularly in Philadelphia, presented a threat to the less prosperous and less populated Delaware. Delaware settlers realized that Pennsylvania would eventually add more counties, which would give Pennsylvania a majority vote in the assembly.

Any bond that did exist between Pennsylvania and Delaware was shattered in 1689 when England went to war with France. Initially Philadelphia feared a French attack, but a decisive victory over the French by an English and Dutch fleet removed that threat. Delaware, however, in its exposed location on the coast, continued to be victimized by French privateers. When Delaware asked for help, the pacifist Philadelphia Quakers refused to come to its aid.

Whether Delaware's separation from Pennsylvania could have been averted if Penn had remained in America is questionable. But certainly by 1699, when Penn

returned after his fifteen-year absence, it was too late. Delaware inhabitants could see the handwriting on the wall. Close to twenty thousand people populated Pennsylvania while Delaware contained only about twenty-five hundred. Both still had three counties each, and Delaware continued to have equal representation, but for how long?

On November 4, 1700, Delaware members of the assembly proposed

> that the Union [of Delaware and Pennsylvania] shall be [re]confirmed on Condition, that at no Time hereafter the number of Representatives of the People . . . in the Province [Pennsylvania], shall exceed them of the annexed Counties [Delaware]; but if hereafter more Counties be made in the Province [Pennsylvania], and thereby more Representatives be added, that then the Union shall cease.[81]

Delaware and the Charter of Privileges

William Penn did not want the union between Delaware and Pennsylvania to end. "I struggle for that poor country's [Delaware's] preservation to the wasting of my time and purse,"[82] he wrote. The Charter of Privileges reflected Penn's sentiments by allowing Delaware three years to decide if it truly wanted a separate assembly. According to the stipulation,

> If the Representatives of the Province [Pennsylvania] and Territories [Delaware] shall not hereafter agree to Joyn

together in Legislation . . . [then] at any time within three years . . . the Inhabitants of Each County in the Territories [Delaware] shall have as many persons to Represent them in a Distinct [separate] Assembly . . . as shall be by them Requested.[83]

DELAWARE LEAVES THE PENNSYLVANIA ASSEMBLY

In 1704 Delaware exercised its right to elect a separate assembly. On November 22 the first independent Delaware assembly met at New Castle. However, Dela-

---

BENJAMIN FRANKLIN ARRIVES IN PENNSYLVANIA

Benjamin Franklin arrived in Philadelphia from Boston on a Sunday morning in 1715, just three years before its founder, William Penn, died in England. In his autobiography, Franklin describes his first day in Philadelphia.

"I was in my working dress. . . . I was dirty from my journey; my pockets were stuff'd out with shirts and stockings, and I knew no soul nor where to look for lodging. I was . . . very hungry; and my whole stock of cash consisted of a Dutch dollar. . . .

I walked up the street, gazing about till . . . I met a boy with bread . . . . I went immediately to the baker's he directed me to, in Second-street, and ask'd for bisket, intending [to get] such as we had in Boston; but they, it seems, were not made in Philadelphia. Then I asked for a three-penny loaf, and was told they had none such. So not . . . knowing the difference of money . . . nor the names of his bread, I bad [bade] him give me three-penny worth of any sort. He gave me . . . three great puffy rolls. I was surpriz'd at the quantity, but took it, and having no room in my pockets, walk'd off with a roll under each arm, and eating the other. . . .

Thus refreshed, I walked again up the street, which by this time had many clean-dressed people in it, who were all walking the same way. I joined them, and thereby was led into the great meeting-house of the Quakers near the market. I sat down among them, and, after looking round awhile and hearing nothing said, being very drowsy thro' labor and want of rest the preceding night, I fell fast asleep, and continued so till the meeting broke up, when one [a Quaker] was kind enough to rouse me. This was, therefore, the first house I was in, or slept in, in Philadelphia."

---

ware and Pennsylvania would continue to share the same governor until after the American Revolution. Historian Charles M. Andrews describes Delaware's distinct status:

> Except for the person of the governor, the separation from Pennsylvania was complete. The new colony . . . was unique in that its right to exist rested on no charter from the crown. It was never obliged to send its laws to England and its affairs very rarely came to the [attention] of the authorities there. . . . No separate file of Delaware papers was ever set apart in the Plantation Office and no seal was ever prepared by the royal engraver in England for Delaware's exclusive use.[84]

Delaware officially remained in the hands of the Penn family until the Revolutionary War, but for the most part, Penn—like England—let the colony go its own way. The little colony that had been shuffled between countries and rulers became America's first state in 1787 when its representatives were the first to approve the U.S. Constitution.

Georgia was unique. It was the only colony established in the eighteenth century. And the reasons for its founding—a combination of military and humanitarian motives—were unlike those of any of the other twelve colonies. In his documentary history *Georgia Voices,* historian Spencer B. King Jr. writes, "Georgia was born in conflict. The eighteenth century witnessed a great drama in the conflict between Spain, France, and England for possession of North America, and part of that drama took place in Georgia."[85]

By the early 1700s England controlled the Atlantic seaboard, except for Florida, which belonged to Spain. Both England and Spain claimed the unsettled area between Florida and South Carolina that would become Georgia. By 1730 English leaders realized that they needed a well-armed colony in this disputed area for the protection of South Carolina. At about that same time, a group of humanitarian-minded Englishmen led by General James Oglethorpe proposed founding a colony for England's unemployed poor.

JAMES OGLETHORPE, HUMANITARIAN

In eighteenth-century England people were sent to debtors' prisons for failing to pay their debts, which were often relatively trivial amounts. A friend of James Oglethorpe died in one of these prisons. Angered by his friend's death, Oglethorpe demanded that Parliament investigate conditions in debtors' prisons. This investigation resulted in the release of ten thousand debtors from prison. Unfortunately, no one would employ them because they still owed money.

Oglethorpe wanted to establish a colony where these people could go to start a new life. He persuaded twenty prominent Englishmen to join him in petitioning the government for the unsettled land south of South Carolina. The Crown saw this as a twofold opportunity: It would solve the need for a buffer colony between South Carolina and Spanish Florida, and it would rid England of its unemployed.

Consequently, the Crown granted a charter to the twenty-one men, empowering them to establish the colony of Georgia. The men were called trustees. Unlike proprietors, they could not own land, hold office, or receive any "salary, fee, perquisite [privilege], benefit or profit whatsoever."[86] They received full governing rights for a period of twenty-one years, after which time the colony was to be returned to the Crown.

WHO WOULD GO?

The trustees envisioned Georgia as a reform colony for rehabilitating people who had been victimized either economically or through a harsh justice system. But the monarchy wanted Georgia to be a self-sustaining military colony, which resulted in a mixed group of carefully screened soldier-settlers.

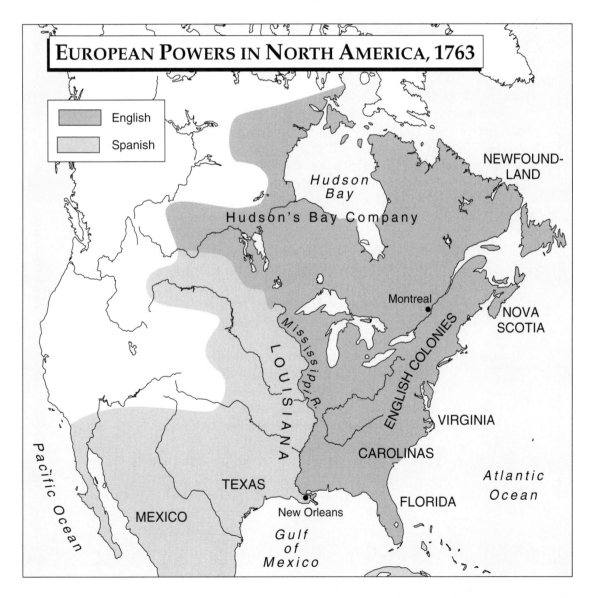

EUROPEAN POWERS IN NORTH AMERICA, 1763

English
Spanish

Hudson Bay
Hudson's Bay Company
NEWFOUND-LAND
Montreal
NOVA SCOTIA
Mississippi R.
LOUISIANA
ENGLISH COLONIES
VIRGINIA
CAROLINAS
Atlantic Ocean
TEXAS
New Orleans
FLORIDA
MEXICO
Gulf of Mexico
Pacific Ocean

The group included a number of skilled workmen and their servants. Certain "worthy poor"—called charity colonists because their way was paid by the trustees—were also selected. One of the trustees described the selection process in his diary:

OGLETHORPE BRINGS SETTLERS TO GEORGIA

Oglethorpe made a trip to England in 1735 to secure additional settlers for Georgia. Among those who returned with him was an English traveler and writer who wrote an account of the voyage to Georgia. His account is excerpted from Georgia Voices *by Spencer B. King Jr.*

"We had prayers twice a day. . . . Mr. Oglethorpe shewed no discountenance [disapproval] to any for being of different persuasions in religion. The Dissenters, of which there were many on board, particularly the Germans, sung psalms and served God in their own way. . . .

All those who came upon the Trust's account [charity colonists] were divided into masses; and besides ship's provisions, the Trustees were so careful of the poor people's health, that they put on board turnips, carrots, potatoes, and onions, which were given out with the salt meat, and contributed greatly to prevent the scurvy. The ship was divided into cabins, with gang-ways, which we call streets between them. The people were disposed into these by families; the single men were put by themselves. Each cabin had its door and partition. Whenever the weather would permit, the ship was cleaned between decks and washed with vinegar, which kept the place very sweet and healthy. There were constables appointed to prevent any disorders, and everything was carried [on] so easily, that during the whole voyage there was no occasion for punishing any one, excepting a boy who was whipped for stealing turnips.

When the weather permitted, the men were exercised [drilled] with small arms. . . . The women . . . employed their leisure time in making stockings and caps for their family. . . .

Mr. Oglethorpe, when occasion offered, called together all those who were designed to be freeholders [landowners], recommended to them in what manner to behave themselves, acquainted them of the nature of the country, and how to settle it advantageously."

We noted down some poor persons who . . . desired very urgently to go over, but we dismissed several who were able to earn their bread in England, and [we] are Careful not to send any who do not satisfy us that they have their creditors leave [permission] to go, and that they do not run away from their wives and families to leave them a burthen on the parish.[87]

BOUND FOR GEORGIA

Oglethorpe would lead the expedition from England to Georgia. Acting as an agent for the other trustees who remained in England, he would function as Georgia's governor. His power, however, was limited.

On November 17, 1732, Oglethorpe and 114 to 120 passengers (records disagree on the number) sailed for Georgia aboard the *Ann*. They reached Yamacraw Bluff located on the slow-moving Savannah River on February 1, 1733, and established the town of Savannah.

RULES, REGULATIONS, AND LAND GRANTS

The trustees planned Georgia as an ideal colony composed primarily of hardworking, virtuous farmers. A posted notice summed up their noble intentions, stating that in Georgia "*Negroes* and *Rum* are prohibited to be used . . . [and no] *Trade with the Indians* [allowed], unless Licensed."[88]

The trustees banned slavery partly because of their own humanitarianism, but they also believed that the moral benefits of hard labor would be lost to the settlers if someone else did their work. The law forbidding rum resulted from the behavior of settlers in other colonies who often sold liquor to the Indians and then cheated them in land deals.

While the building of Savannah was in progress, Oglethorpe turned his attention to establishing a friendly relationship with the Yamacraw Indians—one of the Creek tribes. He met with the Creek chieftain and set up an agreement regarding land and trade. At that time he also purchased the land for Savannah.

The distribution of land was carefully regulated to discourage development of large plantations. Grants could not exceed five hundred acres. (Charity colonists received only twenty acres each.) Women were neither granted land nor were allowed to inherit it from their husbands. This was to ensure that only those who could contribute to the colony's military defense owned land.

There was no self-government in Georgia and the trustees made no provision for a representative assembly. Oglethorpe ruled the colony as a kindly father figure. The charity colonists even called him "Father."

EARLY DAYS

Upon arrival at Yamacraw Bluff, Oglethorpe called the site of Savannah a "healthy Situation."[89] But illnesses like dysentery, influenza, and scurvy soon

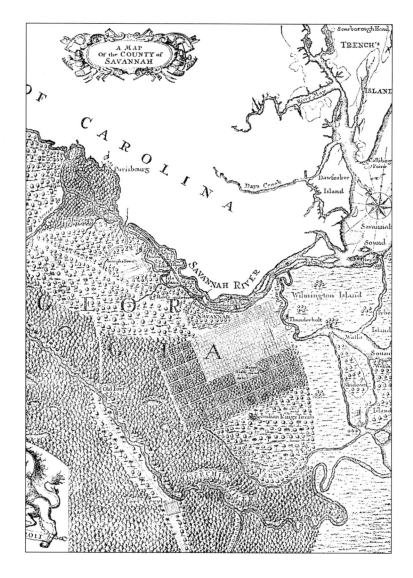

Georgia was originally founded as a buffer zone to protect the Carolinas from the Spanish in Florida.

struck, and death became common. The first to die was the colony's only physician. By the fall of 1733, when the stifling Georgia heat finally gave way to cooler days, one out of every nine settlers had died.

In the meantime, other colonists had arrived. Because the colony had been well publicized, it attracted a variety of ethnic groups, including Swiss, Italians, Germans, Scottish Highlanders, and Welshmen. The Georgia charter had granted religious toleration to all Protestant Christians, but it had excluded Catholics and Jews. Nevertheless, a group of Jews arrived in Georgia.

The trustees in England wrote to Oglethorpe, ordering him to expel the Jews. Oglethorpe ignored the letters and instead welcomed the Jews to the colony, especially when he learned that one of them was a doctor. The angry trustees censured Oglethorpe for his high-handed use of money, for ignoring their letters, and "for doing little or nothing to discourage Jews from remaining in Georgia."[90]

OGLETHORPE SEEKS FINANCIAL HELP

In June 1734 Oglethorpe returned to England to secure more settlers and to confront the irate trustees. No record exists of Oglethorpe's meeting with the trustees, but he obviously silenced his enemies. A resolution was passed stipulating that "thanks be return'd to James Oglethorpe Esqr [Esquire] for the many and great Services he has done the Colony of Georgia."[91]

Oglethorpe also asked Parliament for money to further fortify Georgia against the Spanish. He pointed out that the safety of Georgia as well as all of British America was at stake. If Georgia fell, he warned, the Carolinas and Virginia would

One of James Oglethorpe's goals was to establish friendly relations with the neighboring Indian tribes.

OGLETHORPE REPORTS TO THE TRUSTEES IN ENGLAND

James Oglethorpe was quick to establish a town and meet with the Native Americans in Georgia. In a letter to the trustees written soon after his arrival, he described the site of Savannah and the friendliness of the local Indian tribe. This excerpt is taken from Georgia Voices *by Spencer B. King Jr.*

"I went myself to the Savannah River. I fixed upon a healthy Situation about Ten Miles from the Sea. The River here forms a Half-Moon, along the south side of which the Banks are about Forty Feet high, and on the Top a Flat, which they call a Bluff. . . . I have marked out the Town and Common; half of the former is already cleared and the first House was begun Yesterday in the Afternoon. A little Indian Nation, the only one within Fifty Miles is not only at Amity [peace], but [is] desirous to be subjects to his Majesty King George, to have lands given them among us, and to [train] their children at our Schools. Their Chief and his beloved Man, who is the Second Man in the Nation desire to be instructed in the Christian Religion."

be next, and one after another England's North American colonies would be lost. Faced with this argument, Parliament granted Oglethorpe generous funding, even beyond the amount requested.

Oglethorpe returned to Georgia in November 1735. But only one year later, after erecting forts and negotiating a temporary peace agreement with the Spanish in Florida, he again sailed for England. This time he sought reinforcements for the Georgia militia. He asked that a company of professional British soldiers be stationed in Georgia. When he said the cost of maintaining the soldiers would run about twenty thousand pounds a year, the request was denied. That response would soon change, however, thanks to an English master mariner named Robert Jenkins.

JENKINS'S EAR

On June 11, 1738, Robert Jenkins appeared before the king. Jenkins, who had been arrested by the Spanish seven years earlier on a charge of smuggling, described for the king his ordeal with the Spaniards. He included the gruesome detail that they had cut off one of his ears, which he had saved to show the king.

The English people were infuriated by such cruelty and demanded vengeance. As a result of the public outcry, Oglethorpe was granted his reinforcements and was also named commander of all of the forces in South Carolina and Georgia. England did not declare war against Spain for more than a year, but when the declaration finally came, it was known as the "War of Jenkins' Ear."

WAR WITH SPAIN

By 1739, when England officially went to war with Spain, Oglethorpe was back in Georgia. As the military commander, his ultimate concern was to drive the Spaniards out of Georgia and South Carolina. In addition, he was ordered to capture St. Augustine, the Spanish outpost in Florida. He managed to keep that city under siege for thirty-eight days, but he eventually had to abandon the effort. Oglethorpe blamed the failure on lack of manpower: "We cannot besiege the Town by Land and Water with so small a Force."[92]

Nevertheless, Oglethorpe did end the Spanish threat to Georgia and the Carolinas. The decisive Battle of Bloody Marsh was fought on July 7, 1742, when Oglethorpe and his men ambushed the Spanish on St. Simons Island. Two hundred Spaniards were killed in this battle, but only one of Oglethorpe's rangers was lost.

DISCONTENT AMONG THE SETTLERS

King George II promoted Oglethorpe to brigadier general for "good service in repulsing

Although unable to capture the Spanish fort at St. Augustine, Oglethorpe was successful in eliminating the Spanish threat to Georgia and the Carolinas.

the Spaniards."[93] But the Georgia colonists, some of whom had been pressing for change since 1738, were not as impressed.

Georgia's population and economic growth had not met its settlers' expectations. As a result, many colonists resented the rules and regulations imposed by the trustees. They looked across the Savannah River and saw South Carolina settlers growing wealthy with little effort because of the African slave labor used there. Georgians also wanted the right to own slaves. In addition, they wanted the limitations on individual landownership removed and the law that forbade importation of rum changed. Moreover, Englishmen in the colony, who were accustomed to self-government, demanded a representative assembly.

Many unhappy settlers had abandoned the colony earlier, and with the outbreak of war with Spain, even more had departed. Given the colony's failure to grow and prosper, the Trustees could not sustain their humanitarian ideals in opposition to the ambitious and land-hungry settlers.

THE GEORGIA CHARTER

The Georgia charter contained six thousand words. The excerpts quoted here, taken from Georgia Voices *by Spencer B. King Jr., explain the mixed motives for founding the colony and the measure of religious freedom permitted.*

"We are . . . Informed that many of our Poor Subjects are through misfortunes and want of Employment reduced to great necessities insomuch as by their labor they are not able to provide . . . for themselves and Families and if they had means to defray the Charge of Passage and other Expenses . . . they would be glad to be settled in any of our new Provinces in America. . . .

They might not only gain a Comfortable Subsistance for themselves and families but also Strengthen our Colonies and Encrease the trade Navigation and wealth of our realms and Whereas our Provinces in North America have been frequently Ravaged by Indian Enemies . . . especially . . . South Carolina which in the late war by the neighboring Savages was laid waste with Fire and Sword . . . we think it highly becoming Our Crown and Royal Dignity to protect all our Loving Subjects. . . .

There shall be liberty of conscience allowed in the Worship of God to all persons inhabiting or which shall inhabit or be Resident within our said Province. And . . . all persons Except Papists [Roman Catholics] shall have a Free Exercise of their Religion."

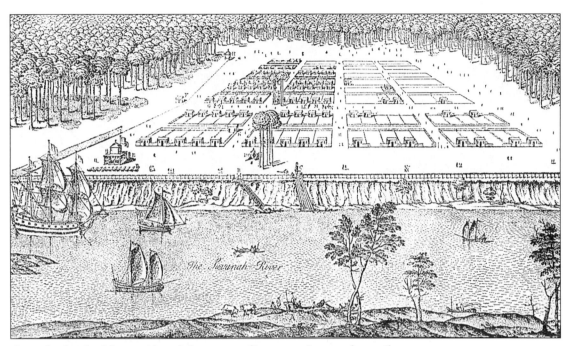

An early sketch of Savannah and the surrounding area. Savannah was the first English settlement in Georgia.

Their first concession was to modify the land policy. Colonists still could not own more land, but they were permitted to rent extra land. The amount of land that could be inherited was also increased, and daughters as well as sons were entitled to inherit. This would lead to the large estates and landed aristocracy that Oglethorpe had sought to avoid. Not long after changing landownership laws, the trustees also repealed the law prohibiting the importation of rum.

THE END OF A DREAM

James Oglethorpe, who had stood firm against colonists who protested his absolute prohibition of slavery in Georgia, left the colony in 1743. With the change in land policies and the legalization of rum, Georgia was no longer the colony Oglethorpe had envisioned. Furthermore, he could see what was coming. After 1745 he rarely attended a meeting of the Georgia Trust.

In 1750, as Oglethorpe had feared, the remaining trustees were forced to surrender the last of their utopian ideals: They removed the restriction on slavery. The colony itself was divided on the issue. While some Georgians opposed slavery, they were outnumbered by its supporters. "The elaborate plans and regulations of the . . . Georgia trustees," historian Darrett B. Rutman writes, "were swept away by men who sought advancement in a fluid society rather than stagnation in a stable one."[94]

MALCONTENTS ATTACK OGLETHORPE

Discontented settlers, seeking repeal of laws prohibiting rum and slaves, put their complaints in a book published in Charleston in 1741. The book, which was a sarcastic attack on James Oglethorpe, Georgia's founder, is excerpted in Georgia Voices *by Spencer B. King Jr.*

"The First Thing he [Oglethorpe] did after he arrived in *Georgia*, was to *make* a kind of *Solemn Treaty* with a Parcel of *fugitive Indians*, who had been formerly banished (by) their own Nation for . . . Crimes and Misdemeanours . . . and all of them have ever since [been] maintained at the Publick Charge [welfare] . . . when many poor *Christians* were starving in the Colony, for want of Bread. . . . A larger sum of Money has been expanded for the Support of those *useless* Vagrants, than ever was laid out for the Encouragement of Silk, Wine, or any other manufacture in the Colony.

Secondly, He *prohibited* the *Importation* of *Rum*, under [the] pretence, that it was destructive to the Constitution [health] and an Incentive to Debauchery and Idleness: However . . . a little Experience soon convinced us, that this Restriction was directly opposite to the Well-being of the Colony."

GEORGIA BECOMES A ROYAL COLONY

Despite all of the compromises made by the trustees, Georgia colonists continued to complain. In 1751, when the trustees asked Parliament for more money for the colony, the request was refused. They turned to the king, but he, too, refused to aid the colony unless the trustees surrendered their charter. Discouraged by the lack of prosperity and the ongoing complaints of the settlers, the trustees surrendered the charter, which was due to expire in two years anyway. In June 1752 Georgia became a royal colony.

As a royal colony, Georgia's government became like that of the other royal colonies with an appointed royal governor and council and an elected representative assembly. Georgia remained one of the poorest of the thirteen colonies, but its prosperity increased under the Crown—not because of the king, but because of slave labor. "Emigration out of South Carolina into Georgia became so universal that year," wrote the king's surveyor general, "that [by 1753] near one thousand

Negroes was brought in[to] Georgia, where in 1751 were scarce above three dozen."[95]

James Oglethorpe never returned to the colony he had founded as a noble experiment to aid mankind. Measured against his high ideals and personal standards, Georgia was a failure. Nevertheless, the last of the thirteen colonies had provided a land of opportunity for many poor and persecuted people from England as well as all of continental Europe.

An Emerging Nation

By the eighteenth century, colonial America had overcome its first growing pains. It had developed into three distinct regions: New England, the Middle Atlantic colonies, and the South. What had begun a century earlier with 114 Englishmen struggling to survive in a strange and hostile environment had grown to nearly 200,000 people. And these eighteenth-century colonists, molded by new influences, circumstances, and conditions, had developed a uniquely American character. As historians Gary B. Nash and Julie Roy Jeffrey write,

> Life in the New World was a puzzling mixture of unpredictable opportunity and sudden turbulence, unprecedented freedom and debilitating wars, racial intermingling and racial separation. It was a New World in much more than a geographic sense, for the people of three cultures who now inhabited it had remade it; and while doing so, they were remaking themselves.[96]

In 1700 little unity existed among the thirteen colonies beyond the common bond of their colonial experience. Colonial America was a mass of contradictions as varied as the people themselves. Loyalty to England competed with a drive for self-government. Slavery existed alongside freedom. And as strange as it seems, the same colonial Americans who allowed the

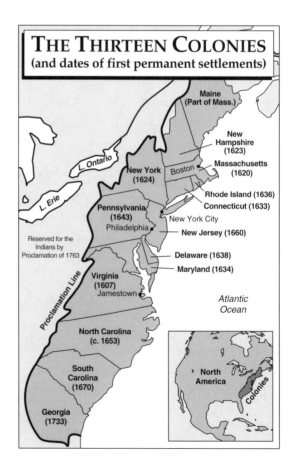

THE THIRTEEN COLONIES
(and dates of first permanent settlements)

Maine (Part of Mass.)
New Hampshire (1623)
Massachusetts (1620)
New York (1624)
Boston
Rhode Island (1636)
Connecticut (1633)
L. Ontario
L. Erie
Pennsylvania (1643)
New York City
Philadelphia
New Jersey (1660)
Reserved for the Indians by Proclamation of 1763
Delaware (1638)
Maryland (1634)
Proclamation Line
Virginia (1607)
Jamestown
Atlantic Ocean
North Carolina (c. 1653)
North America
South Carolina (1670)
Colonies
Georgia (1733)

evil institution of slavery to take root also shared an impassioned belief in individual liberty.

Although colonial Americans made mistakes that would haunt their descendants, they also left a rich legacy of hope and courage. Their democratic ideals formed the heritage that would define America and Americans in the decades and centuries to come. Buried in the mosaic of the different religions, nationalities, traditions, and cultures was the kernel of a great nation.

Revolutionary activist Thomas Paine wrote in 1776, "This New World hath been the asylum for the persecuted lovers of civil and religious liberty. . . . Hither have they fled."[97] Today, people still come to America seeking freedom, seeking hope, looking for their "city upon a hill."

Notes

Introduction: Morning of America

1. Samuel E. Morison, *The Oxford History of the American People*, vol. 1. 1965. Reprint, New York: Penguin Books, 1972, p. 31.

2. Quoted in Darrett B. Rutman, *The Morning of America, 1603–1789*. Boston: Houghton Mifflin, 1971, p. 41.

Chapter 1: Staking a Claim in the New World

3. Morison, *The Oxford History of the American People*, vol. 1, p. 82.

4. Charles M. Andrews, *Our Earliest Colonial Settlements: Their Diversities of Origin and Later Characteristics*. 1933. Reprint, New York: Great Seal Books, 1961, p. 34.

5. Quoted in Warren M. Billings, ed., *The Old Dominion in the Seventeenth Century: A Documentary History of Virginia, 1606–1689*. Chapel Hill: University of North Carolina Press, 1975, p. 21.

6. Quoted in Richard Walsh, ed., *The Mind and Spirit of Early America: Sources in American History, 1607–1789*. New York: Meredith, 1969, p. 13.

7. Quoted in Esmond Wright, *The Search for Liberty: From Origins to Independence*. Cambridge, MA: Blackwell, 1995, pp. 118–19.

8. Quoted in Max Savelle and Robert Middlekauf, *A History of Colonial America*. 1942. Reprint, New York: Holt, Rinehart, and Winston, 1964, p. 85.

9. Quoted in David Hawke, ed., *U.S. Colonial History: Readings and Documents*. New York: Bobbs-Merrill, 1966, p. 69.

Chapter 2: The Fifth Jewel in the Crown: Virginia

10. Quoted in Hawke, *U.S. Colonial History*, p. 71.

11. Quoted in Richard L. Morton, *Colonial Virginia*, vol. 1, *The Tidewater Period, 1607–1710*. Chapel Hill: University of North Carolina Press, 1960, p. 41.

12. Quoted in Morton, *Colonial Virginia*, vol. 1, p. 42.

13. Quoted in Morton, *Colonial Virginia*, vol. 1, p. 52.

14. Quoted in Billings, *The Old Dominion in the Seventeenth Century*, p. 37.

15. Quoted in Billings, *The Old Dominion in the Seventeenth Century*, p. 155.

16. Quoted in Morton, *Colonial Virginia*, vol. 1, p. 69.

17. Quoted in William Dudley, ed., *Opposing Viewpoints in American History*, vol. 1. San Diego: Greenhaven, 1996, p. 22.

18. Quoted in Arthur Quinn, *A New World: An Epic of Colonial America from the Founding of Jamestown to the Fall of Quebec*. 1994. Reprint, New York: Berkeley, 1995, p. 37.

19. Quoted in Marcus Wilson Jernegan, *The American Colonies, 1492–1750: A Study of Their Political, Economic, and Social Development*. New York: Longmans, Green, 1929, p. 59.

20. Quoted in Morton, *Colonial Virginia*, vol. 1, pp. 112–13.

21. Quoted in Morton, *Colonial Virginia*, vol. 1, p. 246.

Chapter 3: Pilgrims and Puritans: Plymouth and Massachusetts

22. Quoted in Jernegan, *The American Colonies, 1492–1750*, p. 124.

23. Quoted in David Hawke, *The Colonial Experience*. New York: Bobbs-Merrill, 1966, p. 125.

24. Quoted in Oliver Perry Chitwood, *A History of Colonial America*. 1931. Reprint, New York: Harper & Row, 1961, p. 92.

25. Quoted in Hawke, *U.S. Colonial History*, p. 89.

26. Quoted in Mortimer J. Adler, ed., *The Annals of America*, vol. 1, *1493–1754, Discovering a New World*. Chicago: Encyclopaedia Britannica, 1968, p. 115.

27. Quoted in Edmund S. Morgan, *The Puritan Dilemma: The Story of John Winthrop*, ed. Oscar Handlin. Boston: Little, Brown, 1958, p. 54.

28. Quoted in Clarence L. Ver Steeg, *The Formative Years, 1607–1763*. 1964. Reprint, New York: Hill and Wang, 1980, p. 39.

29. Quoted in Charles M. Andrews, *The Colonial Period of American History*, vol. 2. 3rd ed. New Haven, CT: Yale University Press, 1939, p. 435.

30. Quoted in Adler, *Annals of America*, vol. 1, p. 172.

31. Quoted in Morison, *The Oxford History of the American People*, vol. 1, p. 167.

32. Page Smith, *A New Age Now Begins*, vol. 1. New York: McGraw-Hill, 1976, p. 49.

Chapter 4: Puritan Offshoots: Rhode Island, Connecticut, and New Hampshire

33. Quoted in Savelle and Middlekauf, *A History of Colonial America*, p. 137.

34. Quoted in Andrews, *Our Earliest Colonial Settlements*, p. 94.

35. Quoted in Wright, *The Search for Liberty*, p. 260.

36. Quoted in Andrews, *Our Earliest Colonial Settlements*, p. 108.

37. Quoted in Charles M. Andrews, *The Colonial Period of American History*, vol. 2, 3rd ed. New Haven, CT: Yale University Press, 1939, p. 88.

38. Quoted in Perry Miller, *Errand into the Wilderness*. 1956. Reprint, New York: Harper Torchbooks, 1964, p. 24.

39. Quoted in Michael Blow, ed., *The American Heritage History of the Thirteen Colonies*. New York: American Heritage, 1967, p. 163.

40. Quoted in David M. Roth, *Connecticut: A Bicentennial History*. New York: W. W. Norton, 1979, p. 44.

41. Quoted in Wright, *The Search for Liberty*, p. 201.

42. Quoted in Hawke, *The Colonial Experience*, p. 151.

43. Jere R. Daniell, *Colonial New Hampshire: A History*. Millwood, NY: KTO, 1981, p. 81.

44. Quoted in Daniell, *Colonial New Hampshire*, p. 92.

45. Quoted in Daniell, *Colonial New Hampshire*, p. 95.

Chapter 5: Catholic Haven: Maryland

46. Quoted in Andrews, *The Colonial Period of American History*, vol. 2, p. 279.

47. Quoted in Chitwood, *A History of Colonial America*, p. 80.

48. Quoted in Andrews, *The Colonial Period of American History*, vol. 2, p. 318.

49. Andrews, *The Colonial Period of American History*, vol. 2, p. 325.

50. Quoted in Andrews, *The Colonial Period of American History*, vol. 2, p. 326.

51. Andrews, *The Colonial Period of American History*, vol. 2, p. 340.

52. Andrews, *The Colonial Period of American History*, vol. 2, p. 372.

53. Quoted in Andrews, *The Colonial Period of American History*, vol. 2, pp. 374–75.

Chapter 6: A King's Reward: The Carolinas

54. Quoted in Hugh Talmage Lefler, ed., *North Carolina History Told by Contemporaries*, 6th ed. Chapel Hill: University of North Carolina Press, 1965, p. 35.

55. Quoted in M. Eugene Sirmans, *Colonial South Carolina: A Political History, 1663–1763.* Chapel Hill: University of North Carolina Press, 1966, p. 33.

56. Quoted in Alexander S. Salley, ed., *Narratives of Early Carolina, 1650–1708.* New York: Scribner's, 1911, p. 69.

57. Sirmans, *Colonial South Carolina,* p. 60.

58. Quoted in Hugh T. Lefler and William S. Powell, *Colonial North Carolina: A History.* New York: Scribner's, 1973, pp. 47–48.

59. Quoted in Andrews, *The Colonial Period of American History,* vol. 3, p. 255.

Chapter 7: A Mixed Bag: New York and New Jersey

60. Quoted in Morison, *The Oxford History of the American People,* vol. 1, p. 121.

61. Andrews, *The Colonial Period of American History,* vol. 3, p. 106.

62. Quoted in Morison, *The Oxford History of the American People,* vol. 1, p. 122.

63. Quoted in Andrews, *The Colonial Period of American History,* vol. 3, p. 113.

64. Quoted in Hawke, *U.S. Colonial History,* p. 172.

65. Andrews, *The Colonial Period of American History,* vol. 3, p. 129.

66. Andrews, *The Colonial Period of American History,* vol. 3, p. 134.

67. Quoted in Andrews, *The Colonial Period of American History,* vol. 3, p. 137.

68. Andrews, *The Colonial Period of American History,* vol. 3, p. 147.

69. Quoted in Samuel M. Janney, *The Life of William Penn: With Selections from His Correspondence and Autobiography,* 4th ed. Philadelphia: Friends' Book Association, 1876, p. 121.

70. Andrews, *The Colonial Period of American History,* vol. 3, p. 156.

Chapter 8: The Holy Experiment: Pennsylvania and Delaware

71. Quoted in Smith, *A New Age Now Begins,* vol. 1, p. 26.

72. Quoted in Janney, *The Life of William Penn,* p. 168.

73. Quoted in Janney, *The Life of William Penn,* p. 178.

74. Quoted in Janney, *The Life of William Penn,* p. 179.

75. Quoted in Janney, *The Life of William Penn,* p. 187.

76. Quoted in Janney, *The Life of William Penn,* p. 259.

77. Quoted in Janney, *The Life of William Penn,* p. 286.

78. Quoted in Janney, *The Life of William Penn,* pp. 351–52.

79. Quoted in Andrews, *The Colonial Period of American History,* vol. 3, p. 319.

80. Quoted in Janney, *The Life of William Penn,* p. 220.

81. Quoted in Edwin B. Bronner, *William Penn's "Holy Experiment": The Founding of Pennsylvania, 1681–1701.* New York: Temple University Publications, 1962, pp. 242–43.

82. Quoted in Andrews, *The Colonial Period of American History,* vol. 3, p. 324.

83. Quoted in Andrews, *The Colonial Period of American History,* vol. 3, p. 322.

84. Andrews, *The Colonial Period of American History,* vol. 3, pp. 324–25.

Chapter 9: Georgia Makes Thirteen

85. Spencer B. King Jr., *Georgia Voices: A Documentary History to 1872.* Athens: University of Georgia Press, 1966, p. 1.

86. Quoted in Webb Garrison, *Oglethorpe's Folly: The Birth of Georgia.* Lakemont, GA: Copple House Books, 1982, p. 46.

87. Quoted in King, *Georgia Voices,* p. 10.

88. Quoted in King, *Georgia Voices,* p. 17.

89. Quoted in King, *Georgia Voices,* p. 11.

90. Quoted in Garrison, *Oglethorpe's Folly,* p. 106.

91. Quoted in Garrison, *Oglethorpe's Folly,* p. 111.

92. Quoted in King, *Georgia Voices,* p. 23.

93. Quoted in Garrison, *Oglethorpe's Folly,* p. 186.

94. Quoted in Rutman, *The Morning of America, 1603–1789,* p. 47.

95. Quoted in King, *Georgia Voices,* p. 30.

Epilogue: An Emerging Nation

96. Quoted in Gary B. Nash et al., eds., *The American People: Creating a Nation and a Society.* New York: Harper & Row, 1986, p. 90.

97. Quoted in Henry Steele Commager and Richard B. Morris, eds., *The Spirit of Seventy-Six: The Story of the American Revolution as Told by Participants.* New York: Harper & Row, 1958, p. 289.

For Further Reading

Leonard W. Cowie, *The Pilgrim Fathers.* New York: G. P. Putnam's Sons, 1972. Traces the early years of the Pilgrims in England and Holland. Re-creates the dangerous voyage of the *Mayflower* and the tiny Plymouth Colony's subsequent struggle to survive. Describes their everyday life, their relationship with the Indians, and the contributions of their leaders. Interesting illustrations throughout.

Jean Fitz, *The Double Life of Pocahontas.* 1983. Reprint, New York: Puffin-Books, 1987. An award-winning biography of Pocahontas, the famous American Indian princess and the roles she played in two different cultures. Describes her hero-worship of John Smith, her kidnapping by the Jamestown settlers, and her subsequent romance with John Rolfe. How she chose between her two worlds is an exciting and engrossing story.

Samuel E. Morison, *Christopher Columbus, Mariner.* 1942. Reprint, Boston: Little, Brown, 1992. This book is based on Morison's Pulitzer Prize–winning *Admiral of the Ocean Sea.* It is the gripping story of a complex man who set out to explore the Indies and instead discovered the New World. The author re-creates the terror and excitement of Columbus's journeys in tiny ships across thousands of miles of unknown oceans as he battled all kinds of weather and an often mutinous crew. An absorbing, fast-moving book.

James E. Seaver, *Captured by Indians: The Life of Mary Jemison.* Ed. Karen Zeinert. North Haven, CT: Linnet Books, 1995. This is the true story of how fifteen-year-old Mary Jemison was dragged from her Pennsylvania cabin by a raiding party of Frenchmen and Shawnee Indians. From that point on, Jemison was an Indian. She was adopted by the Seneca tribe and married a Delaware Indian whom she loved. When the opportunity came to return home, she refused to do so. She recorded her unusual, breathtaking story at age eighty.

Charnan Simon, *The World's Great Explorers: Leif Eriksson and the Vikings.* Chicago: Childrens Press, 1991. Five hundred years before Columbus, Norsemen reached American shores. This book relates the adventures of Norse explorer Leif Eriksson, who left Greenland to sail west into uncharted waters in search of new land. The mystery that surrounds his discoveries make for thought-provoking reading.

Carolyn Kott Washburne, *A Multicultural Portrait of Colonial Life.* New York: Marshall Cavendish, 1994. An excellent work that describes colonial history from the point of view of minorities and women. Numerous maps, photos, and sidebars embellish this well-designed, understandable book.

Works Consulted

Mortimer J. Adler, ed., *The Annals of America*. Vol. 1. *1493–1754, Discovering a New World*. Chicago: Encyclopaedia Britannica, 1968. This first of eighteen volumes contains letters, tracts, documents, poems, and first-person accounts of historical events. Entries address a variety of subjects that range from the well-known Mayflower Compact to the lesser-known Connecticut Blue Laws.

Charles M. Andrews, *The Colonial Period of American History*. Vols.1, 2, and 3, 3rd ed. Reprint, New Haven, CT: Yale University Press, 1939. The author, who is recognized as the supreme authority on colonial America, deals with the English background of the colonizing movement and with the establishment of communities of Englishmen along the Atlantic Coast and on nearby islands. The work is a skillfully told narrative of American beginnings.

———, *Our Earliest Colonial Settlements: Their Diversities of Origin and Later Characteristics*. 1933. Reprint, New York: Great Seal Books, 1961. Examines the three kinds of colonization—commercial, religious, and proprietary—as experienced in five of the early settlements.

Rodney M. Baine, ed., *The Publications of James Edward Oglethorpe*. Athens: University of Georgia Press, 1994. A collection of Oglethorpe's letters, reports, and tracts.

Warren M. Billings, ed., *The Old Dominion in the Seventeenth Century: A Documen-*

tary History of Virginia, 1606–1689. Chapel Hill: University of North Carolina Press, 1975. An outstanding source of letters, documents, laws, and contemporary descriptions of Virginia's first century.

Michael Blow, ed., *The American Heritage History of the Thirteen Colonies*. New York: American Heritage, 1967. Explanatory text coupled with "In Their Own Words" documents and letters of the early settlers. Contains many interesting photographs.

Edwin B. Bronner, *William Penn's "Holy Experiment": The Founding of Pennsylvania, 1681–1701*. New York: Temple University Publications, 1962. A readable chronological narrative of Pennsylvania history between the years 1681 and 1701.

Bruce Catton and William B. Catton, *The Bold and Magnificent Dream: America's Founding Years, 1492–1815*. New York: Doubleday, 1978. An eloquently written history of America from Columbus and the colonial age through the War of 1812.

Oliver Perry Chitwood, *A History of Colonial America*. 1931. Reprint, New York: Harper & Row, 1961. A well-documented, detailed account of the people and events in colonial America. Excellent bibliographical source.

Henry Steele Commager and Richard B. Morris, eds., *The Spirit of Seventy-Six: The Story of the American Revolution as Told by Participants*. New York: Harper & Row, 1958. An outstanding source of British and colonial American letters, speeches, documents, newspaper accounts, broadsides, and pamphlets from 1776 through the ratification of the Constitution.

Wesley Frank Craven, *The Colonies in Transition, 1660–1713.* New York: Harper & Row, 1968. A comprehensive narrative of the significant political, social, and cultural developments in the English colonies on the North American mainland after the restoration of Charles II in England. Includes a helpful bibliographical essay.

Jere R. Daniell, *Colonial New Hampshire: A History.* Millwood, NY: KTO, 1981. A short, succinct, clear account of a colony with a complex history.

William Dudley, ed., *Opposing Viewpoints in American History.* Vol. 1. San Diego: Greenhaven, 1996. A two-volume compilation of speeches, letters, and articles that traces America's social, political, and diplomatic history from its beginnings in Europe. Writings are arranged in a pro/con format, creating a running historical debate on important events and personalities in each era.

Benjamin Franklin, *The Autobiography of Benjamin Franklin.* 1955. Reprint, New York: Washington Square, 1961. Classical work of one of America's most significant statesmen.

John A. Garraty, *Interpreting American History: Conversations with Historians.* London: Macmillan/Collier-Macmillan, 1970. Interviews with acclaimed historians that provide an authoritative overview of American history.

Webb Garrison, *Oglethorpe's Folly: The Birth of Georgia.* Lakemont, GA: Copple House Books, 1982. A clearly written, highly readable biography of both the colony of Georgia and its founder, James Oglethorpe.

Michael G. Hall, Lawrence H. Leder, and Michael G. Kammen, eds., *The Glorious Revolution in America: Documents on the Colonial Crisis of 1689.* Chapel Hill: University of North Carolina Press, 1964. A valuable collection of documents that illustrate the effects of England's seventeenth-century Glorious Revolution on the American colonies. Includes enlightening prefaces by the editors.

Albert Bushnell Hart, ed., *American History Told by Contemporaries.* Vol. I. *Era of Colonization, 1492–1689.* 1896. Reprint, New York: Macmillan, 1925. A useful collection of contemporary documents dating from 1492 through 1689.

David Hawke, *The Colonial Experience.* New York: Bobbs-Merrill, 1966. A comprehensive overview of American history from Columbus's discovery to the ratification of the Constitution.

David Hawke, ed., *U.S. Colonial History: Readings and Documents.* New York: Bobbs-Merrill, 1966. Documents and readings beginning with Marco Polo's report on his travels and ending with James Madison's defense of the Constitution.

Joseph E. Illick, *Colonial Pennsylvania: A History.* New York: Scribner's, 1976. A chronological narrative of Pennsylvania from its beginnings through the American Revolution. Contains a useful bibliography.

Samuel M. Janney, *The Life of William Penn: With Selections from His Correspondence and Autobiography.* 4th ed. Philadelphia: Friends' Book Association, 1876. A somewhat idealized biography of Pennsylvania's founder, but it presents a comprehensive, documented history of the colony through Penn's letters and the author's own narration.

Marcus Wilson Jernegan, *The American Colonies, 1492–1750: A Study of Their Political, Economic, and Social Development.* New York: Longmans, Green, 1929. An old book, it is limited in some respects, but remains useful. Simply written with particular emphasis on the events that produced a colonial society different from that in England.

Spencer B. King Jr., *Georgia Voices: A Documentary History to 1872.* Athens: University of Georgia Press, 1966. A remarkable documentary history of Georgia through letters, broadsides, speeches, and laws enacted. The text is clear, easily understood, and enhances comprehension of the documents quoted.

Douglas E. Leach, *The Northern Colonial Frontier, 1607–1763.* New York: Holt, Rinehart, and Winston, 1966. An informative, well-written history of America's westward expansion. Includes maps, illustrations, and a useful bibliography.

Hugh T. Lefler and William S. Powell, *Colonial North Carolina: A History.* New York: Scribner's, 1973. A chronological history of North Carolina that follows the colony's development from its discovery to statehood. Extensive bibliography.

Hugh Talmage Lefler, ed., *North Carolina History Told by Contemporaries.* 6th ed. Chapel Hill: University of North Carolina Press, 1965. Contemporary accounts illustrating the political, social, and economic development of North Carolina from colonial beginnings into the twentieth century.

Peter B. Levy, ed., *100 Key Documents in American Democracy.* Westport, CT: Greenwood, 1994. Historical documents from 1609 colonial America through 1988.

Paul Robert Lucas, *American Odyssey, 1607–1789.* Englewood Cliffs, NJ: Prentice-Hall, 1984. A well-documented account that describes precolonial Old and New World environments as well as the colonial world of the seventeenth and eighteenth centuries. Extensive bibliography.

Richard P. McCormick, *New Jersey from Colony to State, 1609–1798.* Newark: New Jersey Historical Society, 1981. A brief general survey of the history of New Jersey from its first explorations to the ratification of the U.S. Constitution.

Newton D. Mereness, *Maryland as a Proprietary Province.* 1901. Reprint, Cos Cob, CT: John E. Edwards, 1968. This meticulously researched book addresses all facets of the colony of Maryland: proprietary government, social development, political structure, industrial growth, religious influence, and relations with the mother country.

Perry Miller, *Errand into the Wilderness.* 1956. Reprint, New York: Harper Torchbooks, 1964. Scholarly discussions of Puritan thinking and writings.

Perry Miller and Thomas H. Johnson, *The Puritans.* Vol. 2. 1938. Reprint, New York: Harper & Row, 1963. Source book of Puritan letters, journals, poetry, and treatises. An indispensable guide to understanding the Puritans.

John A. Monroe, *Colonial Delaware: A History.* Millwood, NY: KTO, 1978. A social, economic, cultural, and political history of Delaware from early explorations to the colonial declaration of independence.

Edmund S. Morgan, *The Puritan Dilemma: The Story of John Winthrop.* Ed. Oscar Handlin. Boston: Little, Brown, 1958. An engrossing, vivid account that brings John Winthrop to life on its pages. Entertaining and readily understood.

Samuel E. Morison, *The Oxford History of the American People.* Vol. 1. 1965. Reprint, New York: Penguin Books, 1972. Pulitzer Prize–winner Morison presents a comprehensive history of the American people from the earliest Indian civilizations to George Washington's election as president. A very readable book that is both scholarly and entertaining.

Richard B. Morris, ed., *Encyclopedia of American History.* 1953. Reprint, New York: Harper & Row, 1965. Essential historical facts about American life and institutions presented in a general chronological framework. Information is easily and quickly accessible.

Richard L. Morton, *Colonial Virginia.* Vol. 1. *The Tidewater Period, 1607–1710.* Chapel Hill: University of North Carolina Press, 1960. A well-written, well-researched history of Virginia that takes the colony from its beginnings into the eighteenth century. Includes a useful bibliography.

Gary B. Nash et al., eds., *The American People: Creating a Nation and a Society.* New York: Harper & Row, 1986. A college textbook that provides a comprehensive survey of American history from 1492 into the twentieth century.

John E. Pomfret and Floyd M. Shumway, *Founding the American Colonies, 1583–1660.* New York: Harper & Row, 1970. A history of the settlement of colonies established before the restoration of Charles II in England. Includes an extensive bibliography.

Arthur Quinn, *A New World: An Epic of Colonial America from the Founding of Jamestown to the Fall of Quebec.* 1994. Reprint, New York: Berkeley, 1995. A critically acclaimed literary history of the New World that brings alive the people who explored and opened the North American continent.

David M. Roth, *Connecticut: A Bicentennial History.* New York: W. W. Norton, 1979. A short, readable account of Connecticut's history from colonization to statehood.

Darrett B. Rutman, *The Morning of America, 1603–1789.* Boston: Houghton Mifflin, 1971. A detailed, illuminating study with emphasis on the colonial experience and how that experience culminated in the American Revolution.

Alexander S. Salley, ed., *Narratives of Early Carolina, 1650–1708.* New York: Scribner's, 1911. Contemporary narratives of the history of North Carolina between the years 1650 and 1708.

Max Savelle and Robert Middlekauf, *A History of Colonial America.* 1942.

Reprint, New York: Holt, Rinehart, and Winston, 1964. A sweeping, inclusive history that begins with the European background of America and ends with the signing of the Constitution. Clearly written, highly readable. Includes maps and an incomparable bibliography.

M. Eugene Sirmans, *Colonial South Carolina: A Political History, 1663–1763.* Chapel Hill: University of North Carolina Press, 1966. An engrossing history of the early political history of South Carolina. Written in a clear, concise style that lends itself to understanding. Includes a helpful bibliographical essay.

Page Smith, *A New Age Now Begins.* Vol. 1. New York: McGraw-Hill, 1976. A lively, extensive narrative of America's history written for the general reader. Volume l begins with the first colonial settlers and ends in 1776.

Phinizy Spalding, *Oglethorpe in America.* Chicago: University of Chicago Press, 1977. A well-documented biography of Georgia's founder, focusing on his life in America. Includes a bibliography.

Carl Ubbelohde, *The American Colonies and the British Empire, 1607–1763.* New York: Thomas Y. Crowell, 1968. A clear, condensed history of the relationship between the American colonies and the British Empire up to the French and Indian War.

Clarence L. Ver Steeg, *The Formative Years, 1607–1763.* 1964. Reprint, New York: Hill and Wang, 1980. A history that focuses on development of the American character and on the dissimilarities that developed within each colony. Includes a useful bibliographical essay.

Richard Walsh, ed., *The Mind and Spirit of Early America: Sources in American History, 1607–1789.* New York: Meredith, 1969. Collection of documents that narrates America's early history. Divided into three parts, selections are categorized under the seventeenth century, provincial society, and the Revolutionary era. Enlightening editorial explanations preface selections.

Esmond Wright, *The Search for Liberty: From Origins to Independence.* Cambridge, MA: Blackwell, 1995. A comprehensive study enlivened by vivid descriptions of people and events. Very readable and easy to understand. Contains an outstanding chronology and bibliography together with maps and illustrations.

Index

Africans, 24
Albemarle Sound, 67, 69
Algonquian Indians, 17–20, 22
American settlements by 1770, map of, 24
Andros, Sir Edmund, 41, 51, 79
apprentices
   in Jamestown, 24
   in North Carolina, 72
   in Virginia, 30

Bacon, Nathaniel, 29–31
Bacon's Rebellion, 29
Berkeley, Lord John, 82, 84
Berkeley, William, 29
Blackwell, John, 90, 92
Blaxton, William, 46
Bloody Marsh, Battle of, 105
Bradford, William, 35, 48

Calvert, Benedict Leonard, 66
Calvert, Cecilius, 56
   see also Lord Baltimore (2nd)
Calvert, Charles, 63–66
Calvert, George, 56
Calvert, Leonard, 56, 58, 60
Carolina, 67–68
   see also North Carolina; South Carolina
Carteret, Philip, 82
Carteret, Sir George, 82, 84, 85
Catholics
   conflicts with Protestants, 12, 61

leave England for Maryland, 56
lose power in Maryland, 66
Charles I (king of England)
   beheading of, 39, 51
   encourages commerce in Virginia, 22
   grants Maryland land, 56
   revokes Virginia Company charter, 26
Charles II (king of England)
   becomes king, 63
   colonization during reign of, 67
   death of, 64, 79
   declares New Hampshire a royal colony, 54
   grants Connecticut a royal charter, 51
   grants New Netherland land, 77
   grants Pennsylvania land, 88
   grants Rhode Island a new charter, 45–46
   restores English monarchy, 39
Charleston, South Carolina, 69
Charter Oak, 52
Charter of Privileges, 93, 95–96
charters, significance of, 14
Church of England, 12, 32, 66
civil rights, 37

Claiborne, William, 59–60
colonies
   by eighteenth century, 110
   map of thirteen, 110
   see also specific colonies
Columbus, Christopher, 12
Connecticut
   Fundamental Orders of, 48–50
   Hooker migrates to, 47–48
   organizes into colony, 48
   origins of, 46–47
   Pequot Massacre in, 48
   receives royal charter, 51–52
Council of New England, 52
Cranfield, Edward, 54
Croatoan Indians, 14
Cromwell, Oliver, 39, 62
Culpepper, John, 74
Culpepper's Rebellion, 74–75

Dale, Sir Thomas, 21, 22
Dale's Code, 21
Dare, Virginia, 14
Davenport, John, 49
debtors prisons, 98
Delaware
   becomes part of Pennsylvania, 93–95
   conflicts with Pennsylvania, 95
   early settlers in, 93
   is deeded to Penn, 93
   leaves Pennsylvania

assembly, 96–97
De La Warre, Lord, 19, 20, 21
Dominion of New England
Connecticut refuses to join, 51
formation of, 41, 80
replaces colony governments, 54
Dongan, Thomas, 79
Durant, George, 75

Elizabeth I (queen of England), 13
England
Church of, 12, 32, 66
civil war in, 39
enforces customs fees, 74–75
export duties of, 74
first attempt at colonization by, 13–14
motives of, for colonizing, 12–13
power struggles between Spain and, 12–13, 105
religious conflicts in, 32
second attempt at colonization by, 14–15
views of, toward Quakers, 87
English Bill of Rights, 41
Exeter, New Hampshire, 52

Frame of Government, 88–89, 91
Franklin, Benjamin, 96
freeman, definition of, 37, 50
Fundamental Constitutions, 67–68
Fundamental Orders, 48–50
Gates, Sir Thomas, 19, 20

General Court, 37
authorizes Hooker's emigration, 47
changes in, 41
creates Fundamental Orders, 48–50
resists English rule, 39
splits into two houses, 38
George I (king of England), 76
George II (king of England), 105
Georgia
becomes royal colony, 108
early settlers in, 99–102
founding of, 98–99, 101
map of, 102
political tensions in, 106–107
rum in, 101, 107
slavery in, 106–107
Georgia Charter, 106
Germantown, Pennsylvania, 94
Glorious Revolution of 1688, 41, 52, 83
Goose Creek men, 69–70, 71
Gorges, Sir Ferdinando, 52
Gorton, Samuel, 44
Grand Model, 67–68

Hampton, New Hampshire, 52
Hartford, Connecticut, 48
headright system, 23–24
Henry VIII (king of England), 12
Holland, 32, 78
Hooker, Thomas, 47, 48
House of Burgesses
changes made by, 29

dissolution of, 26
by end of seventeenth century, 31
establishment of, 24
housing, in 1687 Virginia, 28
Huguenots (French Protestants), 70
Hutchinson, Anne, 44

indentured servants, 24, 72
Indian slave trade, 70, 71

James (duke of York)
conquers New Netherland, 77–78
governing style of, 78–79
see also James II
James I (king of England), 56
becomes king, 14
establishes Council of New England, 52
views of, toward Separatists, 32, 33
James II (king of England)
becomes king, 79
flees England, 41
forms Dominion of New England, 39, 41
Jamestown, Virginia
becomes royal colony, 26
burning of, 29
first year in, 17–18
immigrants in, 18–20, 23–25
Indian massacres in, 26, 27
military rule in, 21
settlement of, 15–17
starvation in, 19–20
Jenkins, Robert, 104
Jews, in Georgia, 102–103

Kent Island, 59–60
King Philip's War, 40
King William's War, 53

Laconia Company, 52
Leisler, Jacob, 80, 81
Leisler's Rebellion, 80–81, 83
Locke, John, 67
London Company. *See* Virginia Company
Lord Baltimore (1st), 56
Lord Baltimore (2nd), 56
    appoints brother governor, 58
    appoints son governor, 63
    death of, 63
    instructions of, to Maryland immigrants, 59
    loses control of Maryland, 61–62
    pleads for religious peace, 61
    promotes colonization, 57
    regains control of Maryland, 62–63
Lord Baltimore (3rd), 63–66
Lord Baltimore (4th), 66

maps
    American settlements by 1770, 24
    European powers in North America, 1763, 99
    Georgia, 102
    thirteen colonies, 110
Markham, William, 88
martial law, 21, 23
Mary (daughter of James

II), 65
Maryland
    becomes royal colony, 65
    boundary disputes between Virginia and, 59
    early government in, 58
    first settlers in, 57–58
    is granted to Lord Baltimore, 56
    life during seventeenth century, 64
    political tensions in, 60, 63–65
    welcomes Puritan immigrants, 61
Mason, John, 48
Mason, John (Captain), 52
Massachusetts
    banishes Roger Williams, 44
    becomes royal colony, 41
    boundary disputes between New Hampshire and, 55
    controls New Hampshire, 52, 54–55
    emigrants from, 43
    persecutes Quakers, 87–88
    see also General Court
Massachusetts Bay Company
    charter of, is annulled, 39
    founding of, 34
    government of, 36–38
Massacre of 1622, 26, 27
Massacre of 1644, 26–27
Massasoit, Chief, 40
Mayflower, 33
Mayflower Compact, 33–34
Metacomet, 40
Miller, Thomas, 74–75

Monmouth Patent, 82, 83

Native Americans
    Algonquian Indians, 17–20, 22
    Chief Massasoit, 40
    Chief Opechancanough, 25–27
    Chief Powhatan, 17–19, 22, 25
    Croatoan Indians, 14
    Metacomet, 40
    Penn's kindness to, 89
    Pequot Indians, 38, 48
    Pocahontas, 18, 22
    relations between Pilgrims and, 34
    in slave trade, 70, 71
    Squanto, 34
    Wampanoag Indians, 40, 44
    Yamacraw Indians, 101
Navigation Acts, 39, 41, 74
New England Confederation
    excludes Rhode Island, 44–45
    formation of, 38–39
New England settlements, in 1640, 38
New Hampshire
    becomes royal colony, 54, 55
    formation of, 52
    frontier warfare in, 53
    joins Massachusetts, 52, 54–55
New Haven, Connecticut, 49, 51
New Jersey
    becomes united royal colony, 86
    early settlers in, 82

East, 84–86
land disputes in, 82–83
splits into two parts,
84–85
West
is united with eastern
half, 86
Quaker settlement of,
84–85
Quakers migrate to, 88
New Netherland, 77–78
Newport, Rhode Island,
44
New York
becomes royal colony,
79–80
Dutch heritage in, 78
naming of, 78
political rebellion in, 80
popular assembly in, 79,
82
Nicolls, Richard, 77, 79,
82–83
North Carolina
apprentices in, 72
becomes royal colony, 76
contrasted with South
Carolina, 75
Culpepper's Rebellion
in, 74–75
indentured servants in,
72
insularity of, 68
smuggling activities in,
73–74

Oglethorpe, James
drives Spaniards from
colonies, 105
establishes Savannah,
101–103
humanitarian instincts
of, 98

leaves Georgia, 107
opponents of, 108
religious tolerance of, 100
seeks funds for Georgia,
103–104
Oldham, John, 46–47, 48
Opechancanough, Chief,
25–27
orphans, 30

Penn, William, 84
becomes a Quaker, 87
drafts Frame of
Government, 88–89
is granted land in
Pennsylvania, 88
kindness of, to Native
Americans, 89
returns to England, 90
returns to Pennsylvania,
92–93
Pennsylvania
becomes royal colony, 92
conflicts between
Delaware and, 95
German settlers in, 94
is granted to Penn, 88
political tensions in, 90,
92
proprietary rule in,
92–93
Pequot Massacre, 48
Pequot War, 38
Percy, George, 16, 17–18, 20
Pilgrims
dangers faced by, 35
flee to Holland, 32
relations between Native
Americans and, 34
set sail for Virginia,
32–33
Pinta, 12
pirate trade, 71, 73

Plymouth, Massachusetts,
33–35
Plymouth Company, 14–15
Pocahontas, 18, 22
Portsmouth, Rhode Island,
44
Powhatan, Chief, 17–19, 22,
25
proprietary colonies, 56, 67
Protestant Church of
England, 12, 32, 66
Protestants
conflicts between
Catholics and, 12, 61
French (Huguenots), 70
gain power in Maryland,
66
leave England for
Maryland, 56
Providence, Rhode Island,
44
Puritan Commonwealth,
61–62
Puritans
behead Charles I, 51
elect governor of
Massachusetts, 36
establish power in
Maryland, 61–62
form Massachusetts Bay
Company, 34
lose control in
Massachusetts, 41–42
migrate to Plymouth, 36
obtain charter from
Charles I, 34
origins of, 32
persecution of, 60–61
seize power in England,
39

Quakers
are welcomed in Rhode

Island, 45
origins of, 87
persecution of, 87–88
settle in West New
Jersey, 84–85
Queen Anne's War, 53

Raleigh, Sir Walter, 13
Randolph, Edward, 39
Rhode Island, 44–46, 87
rice crops, 72–73
Roanoke Island, 13–14, 67
Rolfe, John, 21–22
rum, in Georgia, 101, 107

Saints, 33
Salem witch trials, 42
Savannah, Georgia, 101
Separatists, 32
see also Pilgrims
slavery
in Georgia, 101, 106–107
origins of, 24
in South Carolina, 73
slave trade, Indian, 70, 71
Smith, John, 15, 18
Society of Friends, 87
South Carolina
becomes royal colony, 76
contrasted with North
Carolina, 75
early settlers in, 69–70
Indian uprisings in, 71

minority settlers in,
70–71
political tensions in,
70–71
rice crops in, 72–73
slavery in, 73
Spain, wars with England,
12–13, 105
Spanish Armada, 13
Squanto, 34
St. Augustine, Florida, 105
St. Marys, 57, 60
Strangers, 33
St. Simons Island, 105
Stuyvesant, Peter, 77, 78, 79

tobacco crops, 21–22, 59
Toleration Act, 60–61, 62,
63

U.S. Constitution, 49

Virginia
Bacon's Rebellion in, 29
becomes royal colony, 26
boundary disputes
between Maryland
and, 59
first settlers in, 13
growth of, 26, 28, 31
housing in, 28
Indian massacres in,
26–27

land conflicts in, 28–29
orphans in, 30
Virginia Company
charter is revoked, 26
charter issued to, 14–15
establishes military rule,
21
near collapse of, 22–23
reorganizes under De La
Warre, 18–19
reorganizes under
Yeardley, 23–24
tobacco trade of, 21–22

Wampanoag Indians, 40, 44
War of Jenkins's Ear, 104
Warwick, Rhode Island, 44
Wethersfield, Connecticut,
47, 48
Wheelright, John, 52
William III (monarch of
England), 65
Williams, Roger, 43–46
Windsor, Connecticut, 48
Winthrop, John, 36, 37
Winthrop, John, Jr., 51
witch trials, 42
women, 24, 37

Yamacraw Bluff, 101
Yamacraw Indians, 101
Yeardley, Sir George, 23

Picture Credits

Cover photo: Scala/Art Resource, NY

Corbis/Bettmann, 33, 91, 92

Library of Congress, 8, 10, 13, 14, 18, 36, 42, 45, 53, 75

North Wind Picture Archives, 20, 22, 23,

29, 38, 41, 49, 51, 54, 58, 60, 61, 63, 65, 69, 70, 73, 78, 80, 85, 87, 90, 93, 102, 103, 107

Stock Montage, Inc., 15, 17, 25, 35, 40, 43, 45, 47, 50, 77, 82, 105

About the Author

Bonnie L. Lukes is a freelance writer living in Southern California. In addition to this volume, she has written three other books published by Lucent Books. *The American Revolution*, *The Dred Scott Decision*, and *The Boston Massacre*. Her book, *How to Be a Reasonably Thin Teenage Girl*, was chosen by the National Council of Books for Children as an Outstanding Science Trade Book. She has published essays and stories in a wide variety of magazines and newspapers. Her biography *Henry Wadsworth Longfellow, Americas Beloved Poet* was published in 1998.